Songbook

Authors

Lynn M. Brinckmeyer Texas State University, San Marcos, Texas
Amy M. Burns Far Hills Country Day School, Far Hills, New Jersey
Patricia Shehan Campbell University of Washington, Seattle, Washington
Audrey Cardany University of Rhode Island, Kingston, Rhode Island
Shelly Cooper University of Nebraska at Omaha, Omaha, Nebraska
Anne M. Fennell Vista Unified School District, Vista, California
Sanna Longden Clinician/Consultant, Evanston, Illinois
Rochelle G. Mann Fort Lewis College, Durango, Colorado
Nan L. McDonald San Diego State University, San Diego, California
Martina Miranda University of Colorado, Boulder, Colorado
Sandra L. Stauffer Arizona State University, Tempe, Arizona
Phyllis Thomas Lewisville Independent School District, Lewisville, Texas
Charles Tighe Cobb County School District, Atlanta, Georgia
Maribeth Yoder-White Clinician/Consultant, Banner Elk, North Carolina

 in partnership with

Boston, Massachusetts
Chandler, Arizona
Glenview, Illinois
New York, New York

interactive MUSIC powered by Silver Burdett™ with Alfred Music Publishing Co., Inc.

ISBN-13: 978-1-4182-6270-9
ISBN-10:   1-4182-6270-6

10 18

Adelita

Folk Song from Mexico
English Words by Aura Kontra

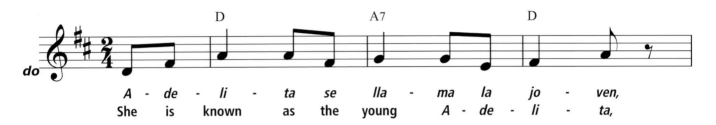

A - de - li - ta se lla - ma la jo - ven,
She is known as the young A - de - li - ta,

A quien yo quie - ro y no pue - do ol - vi - dar.
And she's the one that I love and can't for - get.

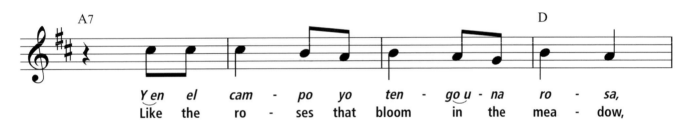

Y en el cam - po yo ten - go u - na ro - sa,
Like the ro - ses that bloom in the mea - dow,

Y con el tiem - po la voy a cor - tar.
Oh, she's the lov - li - est girl that I've met.

1

Adelita

Si A - de - li - ta qui - sie - ra ser mi es - po - sa____
How I wish that she'd mar - ry this young sol - dier.____

—— Si A - de - li - ta fue - ra me mu - jer.____
—— How I wish A - de - li - ta were mine.____

—— Le com - pra - rí a un ves - ti - do de se - da,____
—— Then I would buy her a gown of silk and sat - in,____

—— Pa - ra lle - var - la a bai - lar al cuar - tel.
—— And she would dance through the night at my side.

Arirang

Folk Song from Korea
English Words by Alice Firgau

A - ri - rang,— A - ri - rang,— a - ra - ri - yo,—
A - ri - rang,— A - ri - rang,— a - ra - ri - yo,—

A - ri - rang— ko - ge - ro— nuh - muh - kan - da.
O - ver the— hills— of— A - ri - rang.

Chung - chun ha - nul - en pyul - do— man - ko,—
Voic - es call me from far— a - way,—

I - neh— ka - sem - en— su - sim - do man - ta.
I— must— fol - low,— I— can - not stay.

Arirang

Melody: Reading the Extended Pentatonic Scale

The Ash Grove

Folk Song from Wales

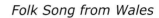

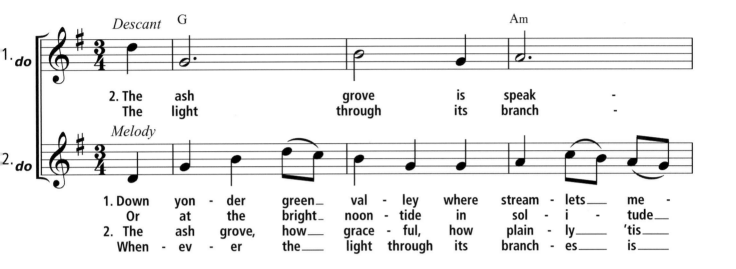

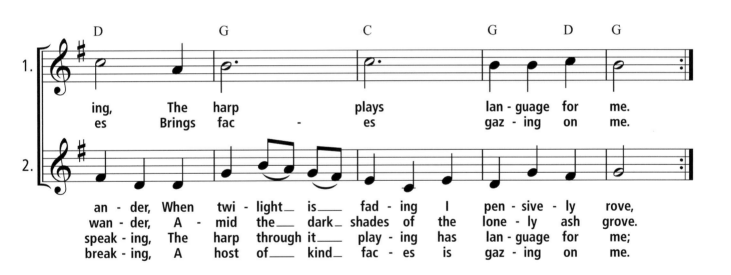

The Ash Grove

(2.) My friends come be - fore me And

(1.) 'Tis there where the black - bird is cheer - ful - ly sing - ing, Each
(2.) The friends of my child - hood a - gain are be - fore me, Each

wak - en mem - 'ries as I roam. Its

war - bler en - chants with his note from the tree. Ah,
step wakes a mem - 'ry as free - ly I roam; With

leaves rus - tle o'er me, The

then lit - tle think I of sor - row or sad - ness; The
soft whis - pers la - den, its leaves rus - tle o'er me, The

ash grove, ash grove is my home.

ash grove en - chant - ing spells beau - ty for me.
ash grove, the ash grove a - lone is my home.

Battle Hymn of the Republic

Music by William Steffe
Words by Julia Ward Howe
Descant by Evelyn H. Hunt

VERSE

1. Mine___ eyes have seen the glo - ry of the com - ing of the Lord;
2. He has sound - ed forth the trum - pet that shall nev - er call re - treat;

He is tramp - ling out the vin - tage where the grapes of wrath are stored;
He is sift - ing out the hearts of men be - fore the judg - ment seat.

He hath loosed the fate - ful light - ning of His ter - ri - ble swift sword;
Oh, be swift, my soul, to an - swer Him! Be ju - bi - lant, my feet!

His truth is march - ing on.
Our God is march - ing on.

Battle Hymn of the Republic

A Big, Wide, Wonderful World

Words and Music by
Sally K. Albrecht and Jay Althouse

With a rock beat

Oh, it's a big, wide, won - der - ful world___ that we live in, a

big, wide won - der - ful world. ___ Oh, it's a big, wide, won - der - ful world

4th time To Coda

___ that we live in, a big, wide, won - der - ful world. ___

1. So
2. From
3. From

PART I

man - y coun - tries,   all mag - nif - i - cent, ___
tow - 'ring moun - tains,   to the flat ter - rain, ___
tor - rid cli - mates,   to the lands that freeze, ___

OPT. PART II

1. So   man - y coun - tries,   all mag -
2. From   tow - 'ring moun - tains, to the
3. From   tor - rid cli - mates,   to the

A Big, Wide, Wonderful World

Blow the Wind Southerly

Folk Song from Northumbria

Blow the Wind Southerly

VERSE

1. He told me last night there were ships in the off - ing, And
2. I stood by the light - house that last time we part - ed, 'Til

I hur - ried down to the deep roll - ing sea; But my
dark - ness came down o'er the deep roll - ing sea; And no

eye could not see it, wher - ev - er might be it, The
long - er I saw the bright bark of my true love, Oh,

bark that is bear - ing my true love to me.
blow bon - ny breeze____ and bring him to me.

D.C. al Fine

California

Folk Song from the United States

1. We've formed our band, we are all well - manned to
2. O!__ don't you cry, nor__ heave a sigh, For we'll
3. As the gold is *thar,* most__ an - y *whar,* And they
4. As__ we ex - plore that__ dis - tant shore, We'll__

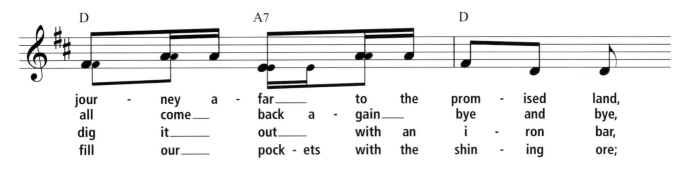

jour - ney a - far__ to the prom - ised land,
all come__ back a - gain__ bye and bye,
dig it__ out__ with an i - ron bar,
fill our__ pock - ets with the shin - ing ore;

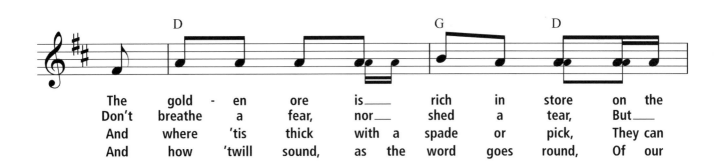

The gold - en ore is__ rich in store on the
Don't breathe a fear, nor__ shed a tear, But__
And where 'tis thick with a spade or pick, They can
And how 'twill sound, as the word goes round, Of our

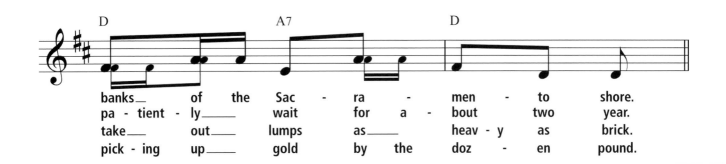

banks__ of the Sac - ra - men - to shore.
pa - tient - ly__ wait for a - bout two year.
take__ out__ lumps as__ heav - y as brick.
pick - ing up__ gold by the doz - en pound.

California

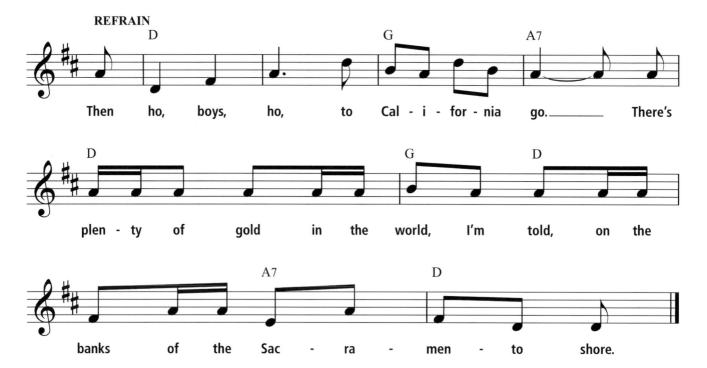

REFRAIN

Then ho, boys, ho, to Cal - i - for - nia go._____ There's
plen - ty of gold in the world, I'm told, on the
banks of the Sac - ra - men - to shore.

5. We expect our share of the coarsest fare
   And sometimes to sleep in the open air,
   Upon the cold ground we shall all sleep sound
   Except when the wolves are howling round.

Camptown Races

Words and Music by Stephen Foster

VERSE

1. The camp-town la - dies sing this song, Doo-dah! doo-dah!
2. The long tail filly and the big black horse, Doo-dah! doo-dah!

The camp-town race - track five miles long, Oh! doo-dah day!
They fly the track and they both cut a-cross, Oh! doo-dah day!

I come down there with my hat caved in, Doo - dah! doo - dah!
The blind horse stickin' in a big mud hole, Doo - dah! doo - dah!

I go back home with a pock-et full of tin, Oh! doo-dah day!
Can't touch bottom with a ten - foot - pole, Oh, doo-dah day!

REFRAIN

Goin' to run all night! Goin' to run all day!

I'll___ bet my mon-ey on the bob-tail nag. Some-bod-y bet on the bay!

Cho'i hát bôi
(The Theater Game)

Traditional Song from Vietnam
English Words by Kim Williams

Rù_____ nhau ra dám kìa mú u kia mú
Wake_____ up! Let's go to the trees, to the

u kia no mú u._____ Cha kêu me_____
grove of mú - u trees._____ The thea - ter_____

hú mày còn ngú_____ tao còn ngú_____ trô'ng linh
game is a - bout_____ to be - gin._____ Hear the

dánh hát bôi dó thúc rôi còn ngôi
drum! It says "come." Wake up! Let's_____

dây sao chang di coi ho hát cho'i.
go, for the play is lots of fun.

Cindy

Folk Song from the Southern United States

A VERSE F   C7

do

1. I wish I was an ap - ple, A - hang - in' on a tree;
2. She took me to her par - lor, She cooled me with her fan,
3. Now Cin - dy is a pret - ty girl, Cin - dy is a peach;

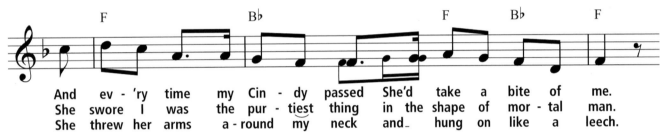

F   B♭   F   B♭   F

And ev - 'ry time my Cin - dy passed She'd take a bite of me.
She swore I was the pur - tiest thing in the shape of mor - tal man.
She threw her arms a - round my neck and hung on like a leech.

F   C7

You ought to see my Cin - dy, She lives a - way down South;
I wish I had a nee - dle, as fine as I could sew,
Well, Cin - dy had one blue eye, She al - so had one brown;

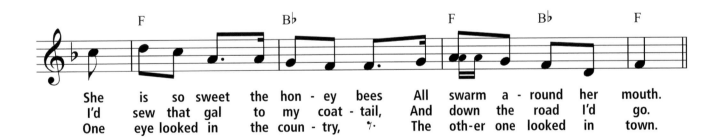

F   B♭   F   B♭   F

She is so sweet the hon - ey bees All swarm a - round her mouth.
I'd sew that gal to my coat - tail, And down the road I'd go.
One eye looked in the coun - try, The oth - er one looked in town.

Cindy

Colorado Trail

Cowboy Song

Eyes like a morn-ing star, cheeks like a rose,

Lau - ra was a pret-ty girl, ev - 'ry-bod - y knows.

Weep all ye lit - tle rains, wail winds, — wail,

All a - long, a - long, a - long the Col - o - ra - do Trail.

Come and Go with Me to That Land

African American Spiritual

swing eighth notes

C7   F

do

1. Come and go with me to that land,_____
2. There's__ no suf - f'ring in that land,_____
3. Peace__ and free - dom in that land,_____

F   Bb   F

Come and go with me to that land,_____
There's__ no suf - f'ring in that land,_____
Peace__ and free - dom in that land,_____

C7   F   C

Come and go with me to that land__ where I'm bound.____
There's__ no suf - f'ring in that land__ where I'm bound.____
Peace__ and free - dom in that land__ where I'm bound.____

20

Come and Go with Me to That Land

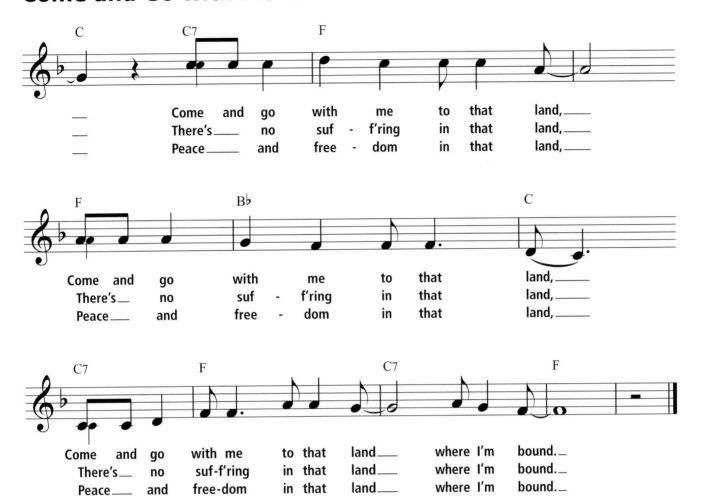

Come and go with me to that land,___
There's___ no suf - f'ring in that land,___
Peace___ and free - dom in that land,___

Come and go with me to that land,___
There's___ no suf - f'ring in that land,___
Peace___ and free - dom in that land,___

Come and go with me to that land___ where I'm bound.___
There's___ no suf-f'ring in that land___ where I'm bound.___
Peace___ and free-dom in that land___ where I'm bound.___

Come Hear the Band!
(A Partner Song with "Alexander's Ragtime Band")

By Irving Berlin
Arranged, with New Words and Music, by
Sally K. Albrecht and Jay Althouse

Come on and hear, come on and hear Al - ex - an - der's Rag - time Band. Come on and hear, come on and hear, it's the best band in the land. They can play a bu - gle call like you nev - er heard be - fore, so nat - u - ral that you want to yell for more. That's just the best - est band what am, my hon - ey lamb. Come on a -

Come Hear the Band!

long, come on a-long, let me take you by the hand, up to the

man, up to the man, who's the lead-er of the

band. And if you care to hear the Swa-nee Riv-er

played in rag-time, come on and hear, come on and

hear Al-ex-an-der's Rag-time Band.

PART II *(or unis.)*

Oom-pah, oom-pah. Hear the tu-ba oom-pah-pah.

The clar-i-nets, the clar-i-nets, doo-dle-oo, doo-dle-

Come Hear the Band!

oo, the clar - i - nets. Ra - ta - ta - ta! The bu - gle call.

Ra - ta - ta - ta! The best of all. That's just the

best - est band what am, my hon - ey lamb.

Ah,_____ ah._____ Hear the trom - bone, ah._____

Come hear the flute. Come hear the flute. Twee - dle - dee, twee - dle -

dee, come hear the flute. If you hear the Swa - nee Riv - er

played in rag - time, come on and hear,

come on and hear Al - ex - an - der's Rag - time Band.

Come Hear the Band!

Come Hear the Band!

Come Hear the Band!

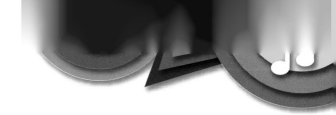

Come, Ye Thankful People, Come

Music by George J. Elvey
Words by Henry Alford

Comin' Up Christmas Time

Words and Music by Joseph Barbera,
William Hanna and Hoyt Curtin
Arranged by Andy Beck

Brightly ♩ = c. 126

1. do — Deck the hall with boughs of hol - ly.

2. do — Jin - gle bells, jin - gle bells,

'Tis the sea - son to be jol - ly.

jin - gle all the way.

Jin - gle bells, jin - gle bells, jin - gle all the way.

It's a - bout that time, that time of the year a - gain.

Comin' Up Christmas Time

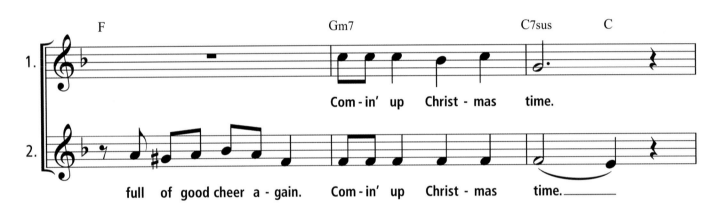

Comin' Up Christmas Time

Comin' Up Christmas Time

Comin' Up Christmas Time

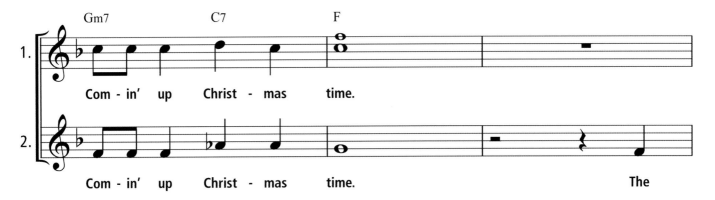

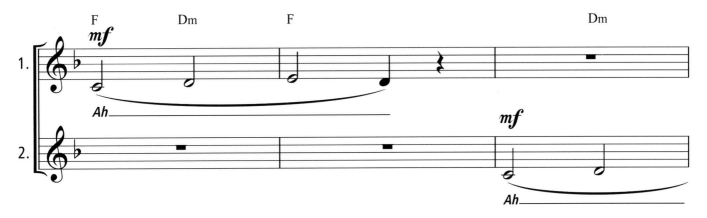

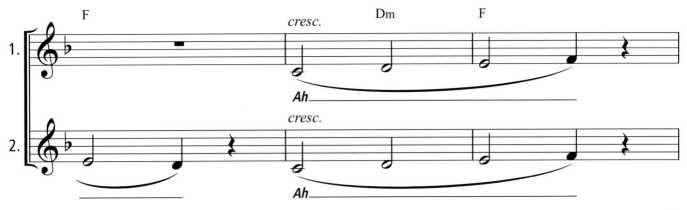

Comin' Up Christmas Time

Comin' Up Christmas Time

Comin' Up Christmas Time

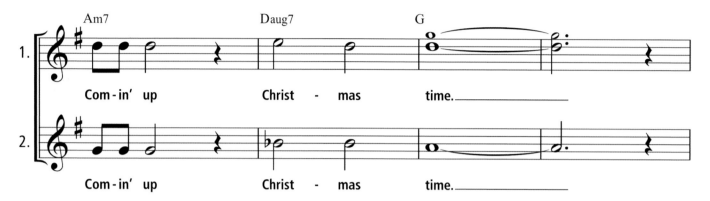

Com - in' up   Christ - mas   time._____

Com - in' up   Christ - mas   time._____

Deck   the hall   with boughs of   hol - ly!_____

Jin - gle   all   the way!

De colores

Folk Song from Mexico
English Words by Alice Firgau

De_____ co - lo - res,_____ De co - lo - res se vis - ten los
When_____ the mead - ows,_____ when the mead-ows burst forth in the

cam - pos en la pri - ma - ve - ra,_____
cool, dew - y col - ors of spring - time;_____

De_____ co - lo - res,_____ De co - lo - res son los pa - ja -
When_____ the swal - lows,_____ when the swal-lows come wing - ing in

ri - tos que vie - nen de a - fue - ra,_____
clouds of bright col - ors from far - off;_____

De colores

De_____ co - lo - res,_____ De co - lo - res es el ar - co
When_____ the rain - bow,_____ when the rain - bow spreads rib - bons of

i - ris que ve - mos lu - cir,_____ y por e - so los
col - or all o - ver the sky;_____ Then I know why the

gran - des a - mo - res de mu - chos co - lo - res, me
splen - dors of true love are great and their col - ors, the

1.
gus - tan a mí._____
best ones of all._____

2.
gus - tan a mí._____
best ones of all._____

Deck the Hall

Traditional Carol from Wales

1.
2. *do*

F

1. ⎰ Deck   the   hall   with   boughs   of   hol - ly,
  ⎱ 'Tis   the   sea - son   to   be   jol - ly,

2. ⎰ See   the   blaz - ing   Yule   be - fore   us,
  ⎱ Strike   the   harp   and   join   the   chor - us,

C7   **F**   **B♭**   **C7**   **F**

1.
Fa   la   la   la   la   la   la   la   la.

Countermelody

2.
Fa   la   la   la   la   la   la.

C7   **F**   **C**

1.
Don   we   now   our   gay   ap - par - el,
Fol - low   me   in   mer - ry   mea - sure,

Deck the Hall

Fa la la   la la la   la la la.

Fa   la la la la la la   la la la.

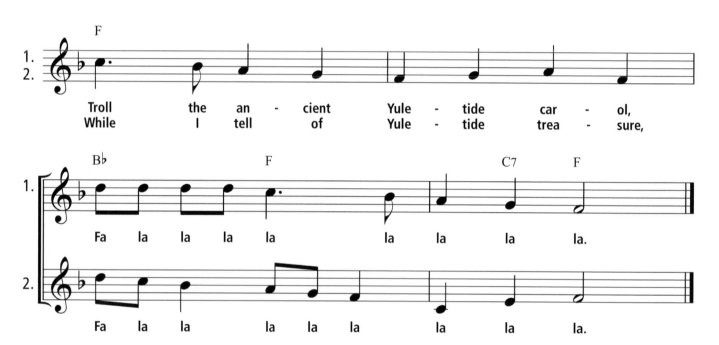

Troll   the an - cient   Yule - tide   car - ol,
While   I   tell   of   Yule - tide   trea - sure,

Fa la la la la   la la la la.

Fa la la   la la la   la la la.

3. Fast away the old year passes,
   Fa la la...
   Hail the new, ye lads and lasses,
   Fa la la...
   Sing we joyous all together,
   Fa la la...
   Heedless of the wind and weather,
   Fa la la...

Don Alfonso

Folk Song from Spain
English Words by Samuel Maquí

1. De los ár - bo - les fru - ta - les___ Me gus -
2. "¿Dón - de vas, Al - fon - so Do - ce?___ ¿Dón - de

1. Of the fruit trees,___ I pre - fer the___ ros - y
2. "In your sad - ness,___ Don Al - fon - so,___ may I

ta el me - lo - co - tón, Y de los rey - es___ de Es -
vas, tris - te de ti?" "Voy en bus - ca___ de Mer -

peach to oth - ers known; And of the kings of___ Spain the
ask where you are bound?" "I must seek my___ dear Mer -

pa - ña,___ Don Al - fon - so de Bor - bón.___
ce - des___ que ha - ce tiem - po no la vi."___

best is___ Don Al - fon - so de Bor - bon.___
ce - des,___ in Ma - drid she can be found."___

3. *Ya Meredes está muerta, Muerta está que yo la vi,*
   Cuatro duques la llevaban Por las calles de Madrid.

3. But Mercedes has departed, she is gone, no more to see.
   She was carried through the city by four dukes of high degree.

41

Down by the Riverside

African American Spiritual

VERSE

G

do

1. Gon - na lay down my sword and shield,____
2. Gon - na join hands with ev - 'ry - one,____
3. Gon - na ring out a song of joy,____

G

Down by the riv - er - side,____

D7

Down by the riv - er - side,____

G

Down by the riv - er - side,____

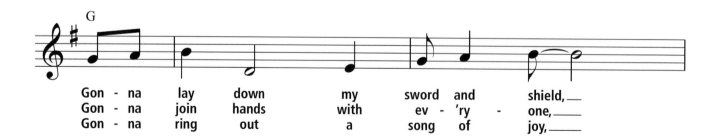

G

Gon - na lay down my sword and shield,____
Gon - na join hands with ev - 'ry - one,____
Gon - na ring out a song of joy,____

Down by the Riverside

Drill, Ye Tarriers

Words and Music by Thomas Casey

VERSE
Cm
do
1. Ev - 'ry morn-ing at sev-en o' - clock There's twen - ty tar - ri - ers a -
2. Our new fore-man is Dan Mc - Cann, I'll tell you sure he's a
3. Next time pay - day comes a - round, Jim Goff was short one
Cm
work - ing at the rock, And the boss comes a - long and he
blame mean man; Last week a prema - ture
buck, he found; "What for?" says he; then
Cm
says, "Keep still, And come down heav - y on the cast iron drill."
blast went off, And a mile in the air went Big Jim Goff.
this re - ply, "You're docked for the time you were up in the sky."
REFRAIN
Cm G7 Cm Gm
So drill, ye tar - ri - ers, drill, And drill, ye tar - ri - ers,
Cm
drill! Oh, it's work all day for sug - ar in your tay,
Cm Gm Cm G7 Cm
Down be-yond the rail - way, And drill, ye tar - ri - ers, drill.

Drill, Ye Tarriers

Percussion

Ego sum pauper

(Nothing Do I Own)

Traditional

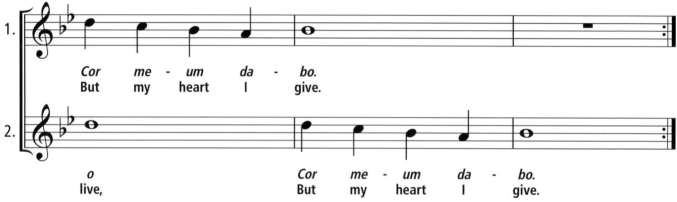

Erie Canal

Folk Song from the United States

Erie Canal

And / 'Cause } we know___ ev - 'ry inch of the way

From Al - ba - ny___ to___ Buf - fa - lo.___

REFRAIN
Response (All)

Low bridge, ev - 'ry - bod - y down,

Low bridge, 'cause we're com - ing to a town;

And you'll al - ways know your neigh - bor, You'll al - ways know your pal,

If you ev - er nav - i - gat - ed on the E - rie Ca - nal!___

Ev'ry Time I Feel the Spirit

African American Spiritual

Frosty the Snowman

Words and Music by
Steve Nelson and Jack Rollins
Arranged by Kirby Shaw

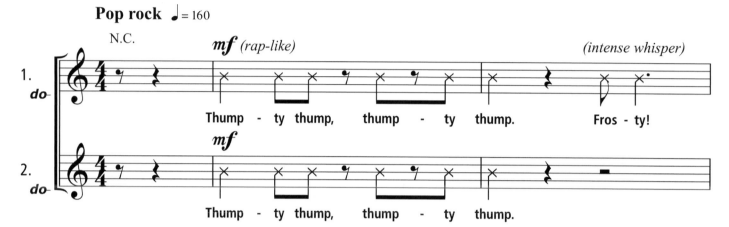

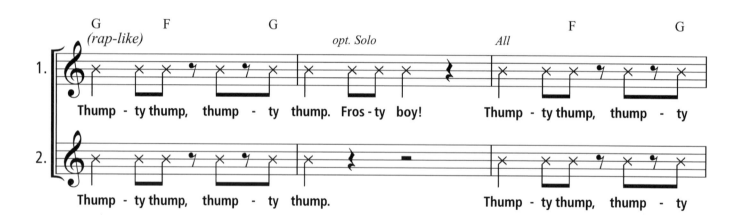

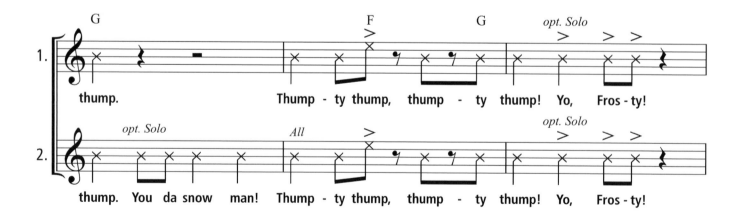

Frosty the Snowman

Frosty the Snowman

Frosty the Snowman

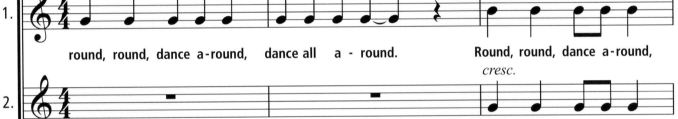

Tempo I

Frosty the Snowman

Frosty the Snowman

Frosty the Snowman

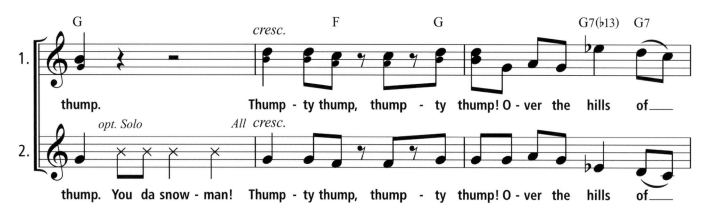

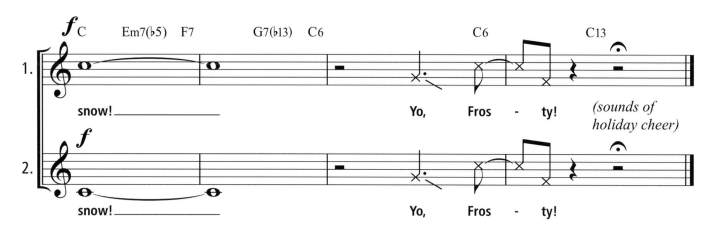

Funwa alafia
(Welcome, My Friends)

Folk Song from West Africa
English Words by Donald Scafuri

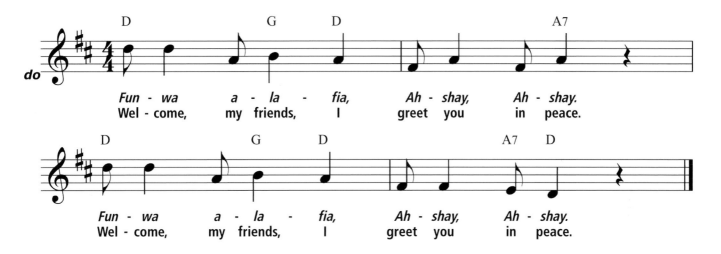

do

Fun - wa   a - la - fia,   Ah - shay,   Ah - shay.
Wel - come,   my friends,   I   greet you   in peace.

Fun - wa   a - la - fia,   Ah - shay,   Ah - shay.
Wel - come,   my friends,   I   greet you   in peace.

Funwa Alafia

Recorder Countermelody

INTRODUCTION

VERSE
3 times

INTERLUDE

Get on Your Feet

Words and Music by John DeFaria,
Clay Ostwald, and Jorge Casas

REFRAIN

Get on your feet. Get up and make it hap-
Get on your feet. Don't stop be-fore it's o-

-pen.___ Get on your feet. Stand
-ver.___ Get on your feet. The

Second time D.S. 𝄋
Third time To Coda ⊕

up and take some ac - tion.___
weight is off your shoul - der.___

1. You say I know___ it's a waste of time.___ There's no use try-

-ing.___ So scared that life's___ gon - na pass you by;___

Get on Your Feet

your spir - it dy - ing. ___ Not long a - go ___
2. I think it's true ___

___ I could feel your strength and your de - vo - tion. ___
___ that we've all been through some nas - ty weath - er. ___

What was so clear ___ is now o - ver cast ___ with mixed e - mo -
Let's un - der - stand ___ that we're here to han - dle things to - geth -

- tions. ___ Deep in ___ your heart is ___ the
- er. ___ You got - ta keep look - ing on - to to -

an - swer. ___ Find it; I know it will pull you through.
mor - row. ___ There's so much in life that's ___ meant for you. ___

Coda

Sing 4 times (with Refrain ad lib.)

Oh ___ way oh! Oh ___ Oh way oh!

(Get) on your feet!

Habemos llegado
(We Have Arrived)

Folk Song from Puerto Rico
English Words by David Eddleman

1. Ha - be - mos lle - ga - do a su a - ma - do ho - gar. Ha -
2. Ói - ga - me, se - ño - ra, le ven - go a can - tar. Ói -
1. We stand at the door of your dwell - ing so dear, We
2. So hark, la - dy dear, to the song that I sing, So

be - mos lle - ga - do a su a - ma - do ho - gar. Con
ga - me, se - ño - ra, le ven - go a can - tar. Que es
stand at the door of your dwell - ing so dear; With
hark, la - dy dear, to the song that I sing; My

con - chas, con per - las, con bri - sas del mar; con
u - na pro - me - sa que quie - ro pa - gar; que es
shells and with pearls and with sea breeze - es near, With
prom - ise to keep is the song that I bring, My

con - chas, con per - las, con bri - sas del mar.
u - na pro - me - sa que quie - ro pa - gar.
shells and with pearls and with sea breeze - es near.
prom - ise to keep is the song that I bring.

Happy Days Are Here Again

Music by Milton Ager
Words by Jack Yellen

A Hero in Us All

Words and Music by
Michael and Jill Gallina (ASCAP)

A Hero in Us All

He - roes, we can all be he - roes,

by do - ing sim - ple acts of kind - ness great and small.

He - roes, we can all be

he - roes, for deep in - side there hides a he -

- ro in us all.____

PART I
He - roes, we can all be he - roes, by do - ing

PART II (opt.)
He - roes, we can all be he - roes, do - ing

A Hero in Us All

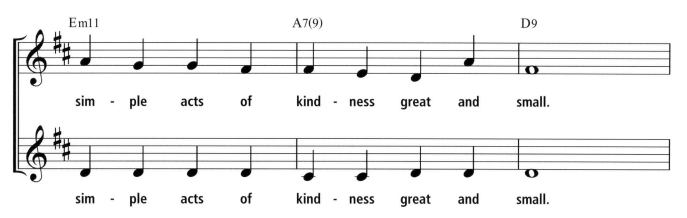

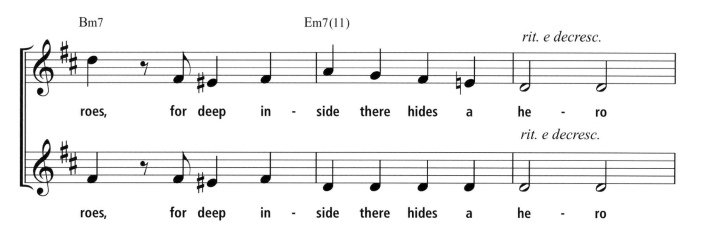

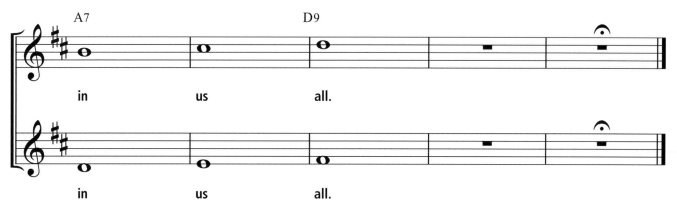

Himmel und Erde
(Music Alone Shall Live)

Round from Germany

I

Him - mel und Er - de müss - en ver - gehn;
All things shall per - ish from un - der the sky;

II

a - ber die Mu - si - ca, a - ber die Mu - si - ca,
Mu - sic a - lone shall live, Mu - sic a - lone shall live,

III

a - ber die Mu - si - ca blei - bet be - stehn.
Mu - sic a - lone shall live, nev - er to die.

Hip-Hop Reindeer

Words by Andy Beck and Brian Fisher
Music by Andy Beck

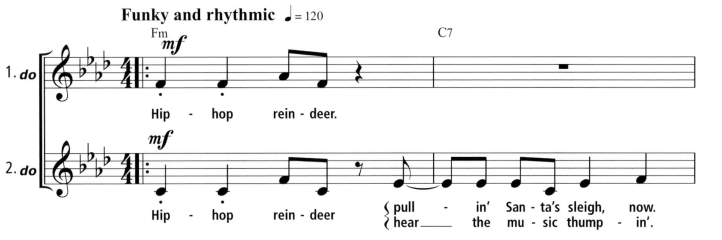

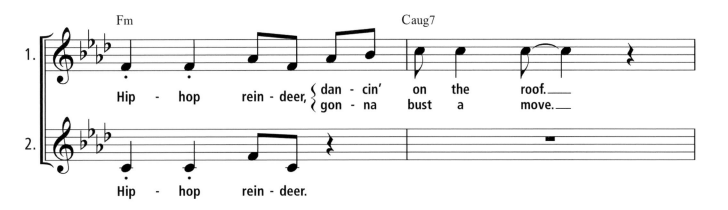

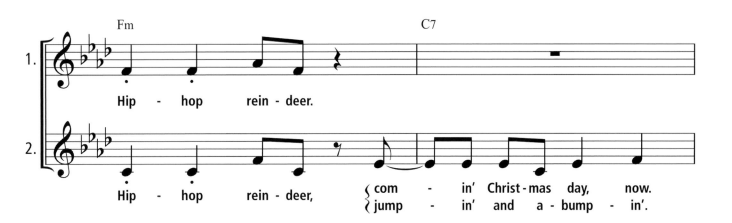

Hip-Hop Reindeer

1. Hear the clat - ter of ev - 'ry hoof.___
   Ev - 'ry - bod - y is in the groove.___

2. Hear the clat - ter of ev - 'ry hoof.___
   Ev - 'ry - bod - y is in the groove.___

1. Dash - er and Danc - er, and Pranc - er, and Vix - en,

2. Com - et, and Cu - pid, and Don - ner, and Blitz - en,

1. break - in', and shak - in', there is no mis - tak - in'

2. break - in', and shak - in', there is no mis - tak - in'

Hip-Hop Reindeer

Hip-Hop Reindeer

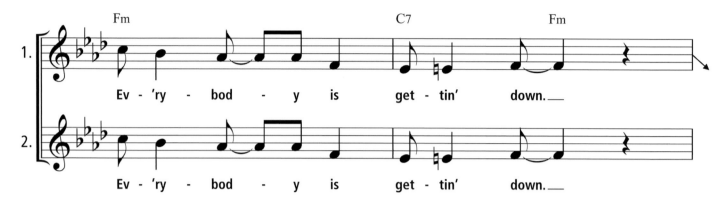

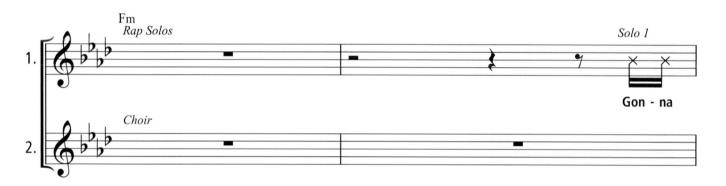

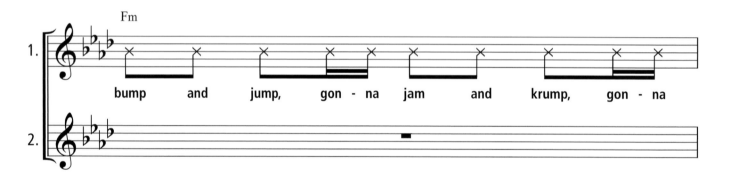

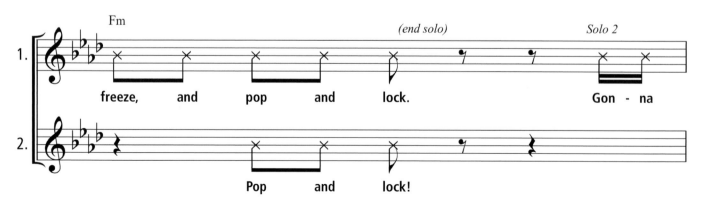

Hip-Hop Reindeer

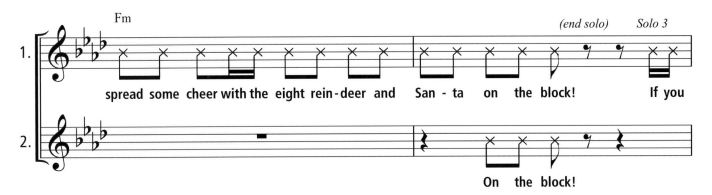

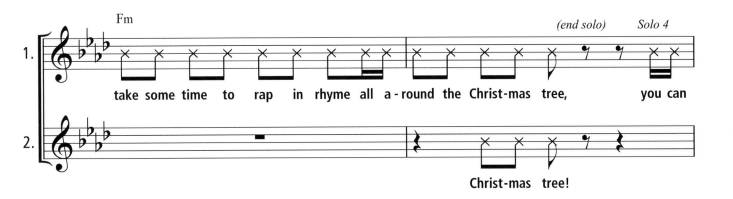

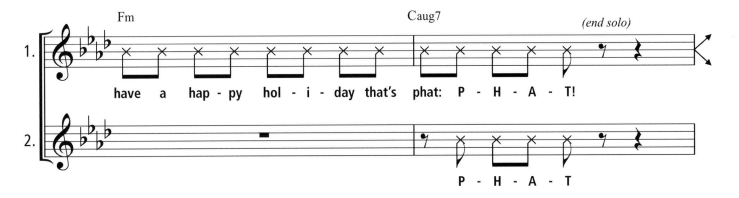

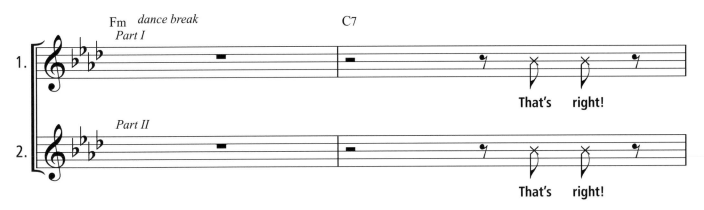

Hip-Hop Reindeer

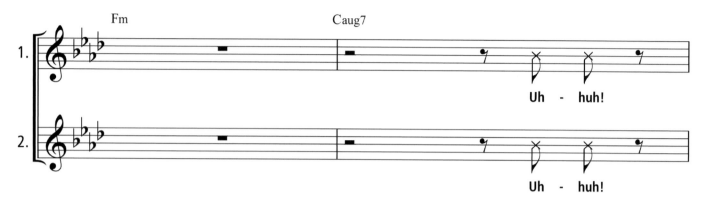

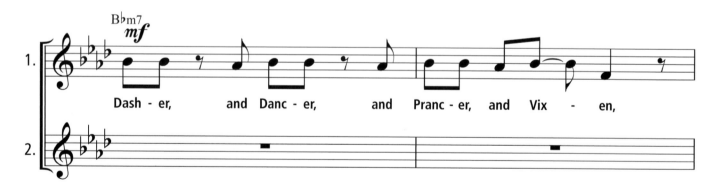

Hip-Hop Reindeer

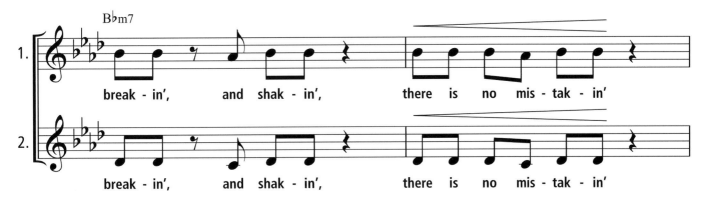

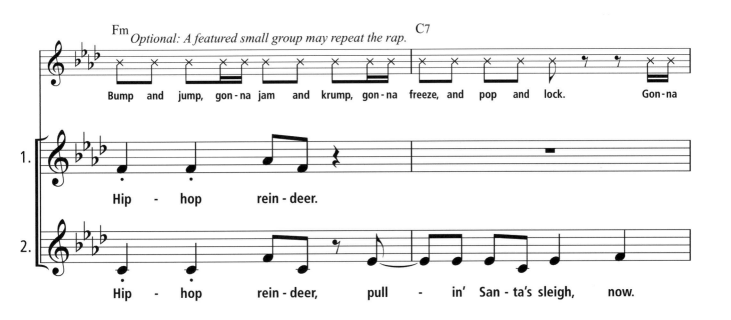

Hip-Hop Reindeer

Hip-Hop Reindeer

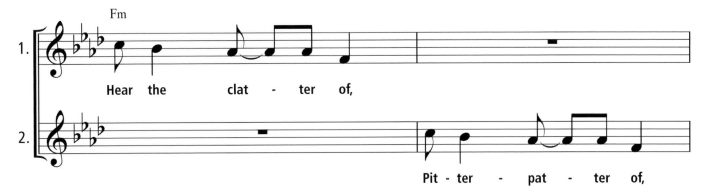

1. Hear the clat - ter of,

2. Pit - ter - pat - ter of,

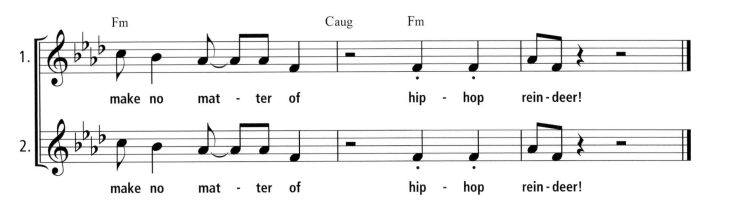

1. make no mat - ter of hip - hop rein - deer!

2. make no mat - ter of hip - hop rein - deer!

Hitotsu toya
(Temple Bells)

Folk Song from Japan
English Words Anonymous

1. Hi - to - tsu to - ya, _____ Hi - to - yo a - ku - re - ba
1. Tem - ple bells will chime, oh, _____ chime for the bright new year that
2. Fu - ta - tsu to - ya, _____ Fu - ta - ba no ma - tsu wa
2. Tem - ple bells will chime, oh, _____ chime for the fra - grance and the

Ni - gi - ya - ka de, Ni - gi - ya - ka de,
comes to us to - night, Comes to us to - night.
I - ro yo _____ te, I - ro yo _____ te.
green through - out the year, green through - out the year.

O - ka - za - ri ta - te ta - ru Ma - tsu - ka - za -
Now on ev - 'ry door there hangs a spray of love - ly
Sa - n - ga - i - ma - tsu wa Ka - su - ga ya -
Of the fine and health - y pine on Ka - su - ga Ya -

ri, _____ Ma - tsu - ka - za - ri.
pine, a _____ spray of love - ly pine.
ma, _____ Ka - su - ga ya - ma.
ma, on _____ Ka - su - ga Ya - ma.

3. Mittsu toya,
   Minasan kono hi wa
   Raku-asobi, Raku-asobi,
   Furusaki komado de
   Hane o tsuku, Hane o tsuku.

3. Temple bells will chime, oh,
   chime in the merriment, the
   music, games, and dance,
   music, games, and dance.
   People swing the battledore.
   This is the time to play.
   This is the day to play.

Hosanna, Me Build a House

Calypso Song from Jamaica

1. Ho - san - na, me build a house, oh,___ Ho -
san - na, me build a house, oh,___ Ho - san - na, me build a
house, oh,___ I built it on the san - dy ground. Me
house built on a san - dy ground, It will fall, you see. Me
house built with sand all 'round, It will fall, you see. The
rain will___ wet it up (ha, ha), The sun will burn it___ up (ha, ha), The
breeze will shake it___ up (ha, ha), The storm come blow it___

Hosanna, Me Build a House

down (ha, ha). Me house can nev-er___ be (no, no), Me

house too weak, you___ see (no, no), Me house will not stand

(no, no),___ Storm blow it on-to the ground (ha, ha).

2. Ho - san - na, me build a house, oh,___ Ho -

san - na, me build a house, oh,___ Ho - san - na, me build a

house, oh,___ I built it on the sol - id ground. Me

house built on a sol - id ground, It - 'll stand up, you

Hosanna, Me Build a House

How Lucky You Are
(*from* Seussical the Musical)

Lyrics by Lynn Ahrens
Music by Stephen Flaherty
Arranged by Andy Beck

How Lucky You Are

I Love a Piano

Words and Music by Irving Berlin
Arranged by Robert W. Smith

I love a pia-no, I love a pia-no, I love to

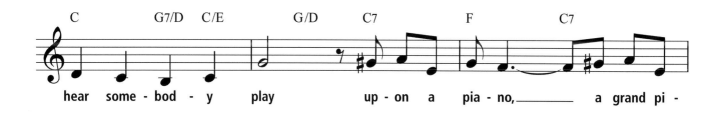

hear some-bod-y play up-on a pia-no,_____ a grand pi-

an - o,_____ it sim-ply car-ries me a - way.

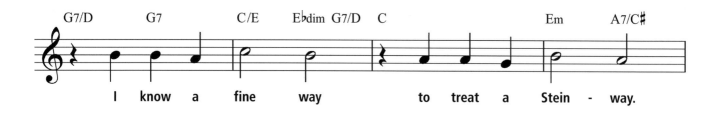

I know a fine way to treat a Stein - way.

I love to run my fin-gers o'er the keys,___ the i - vo - ries. And with the

I Love a Piano

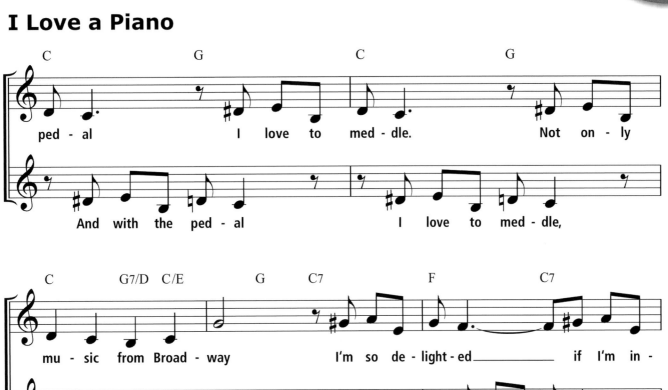

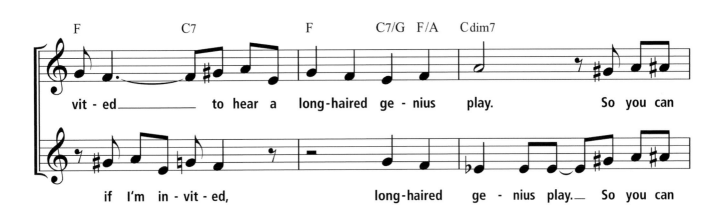

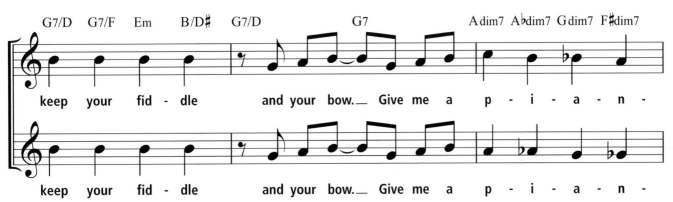

I Love a Piano

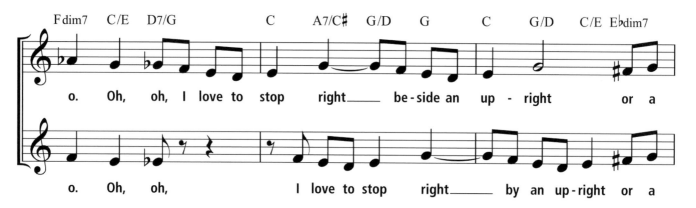

o. Oh, oh, I love to stop right_____ be-side an up-right or a

o. Oh, oh, I love to stop right_____ by an up-right or a

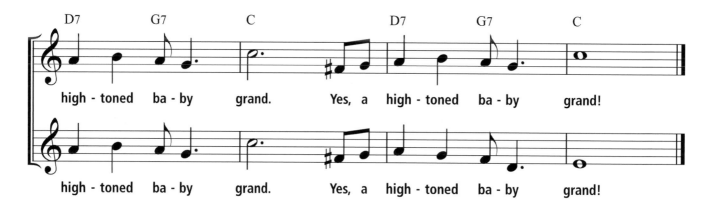

high - toned ba - by grand. Yes, a high - toned ba - by grand!

high - toned ba - by grand. Yes, a high - toned ba - by grand!

I Love the Mountains

Traditional

do

F   Dm   Gm   C7

I love the moun - tains, I love the roll - ing hills,

F   Dm   Gm   C7

I love the flow - ers, I love the daf - fo - dils,

F   Dm   Gm   C7

I love the fire - side, When all the lights are low,

Last time

F   Dm   Gm   C7   F

Boom - dee-ah - da, boom - dee-ah - da, Boom - dee - ah - da, boom - dee - ah - da, Boom!

I Love the Mountains

Rhythm: Reading Dotted-Rhythm Patterns

Last time

I Vow to You, My Country

Melody by Gustav Holst
Arranged by R. Osborne
Words by Sir Cecil Spring-Rice

1. I vow to you, my coun - try, all earth - ly things a -

bove, En - tire and whole and per - fect, the ser - vice of my

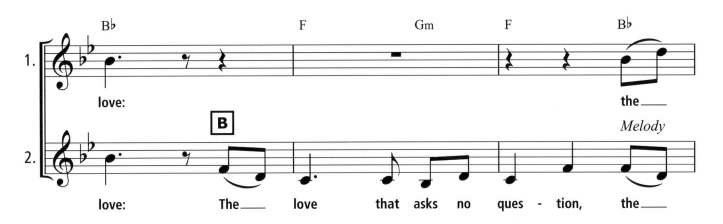

1. love: the

2. love: The love that asks no ques - tion, the

1. love that stands the test, That lays up - on the al - tar the

2. love that stands the test, That lays up - on the al - tar the

I Vow to You, My Country

I Vow to You, My Country

I Vow to You, My Country

ev - er reign su - preme;   And when time   stands still,   my   home - land,   may

ev - er reign su - preme;   And when time   stands still,   my   home - land,   may

heav - en   hold   your   dream.   Home - land.

heav - en   hold   your   dream.   Home - land.

I've Been Everywhere

Words and Music by Geoff Mack
Arranged by Jay Althouse

I've Been Everywhere

I've Been Everywhere

I've Been Everywhere

where.

where.

I've been to Re - no, Chi - ca - go, Far - go, Min - ne - so - ta,

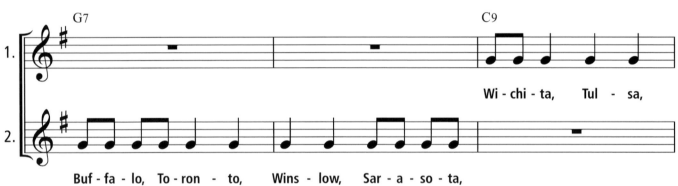

Wi - chi - ta, Tul - sa,

Buf - fa - lo, To - ron - to, Wins - low, Sar - a - so - ta,

Ot - ta - wa, Ok - la - ho - ma,

Tam - pa, Pa - na - ma, Mat - ta - wa, La Pa - lo - ma,

Ban - gor, Bal - ti - more, Sal - va - dor, Am - a - ril - lo,

To - ca - pil - lo, Bar - ran - quil - la,

I've Been Everywhere

I've Been Everywhere

I've Been Everywhere

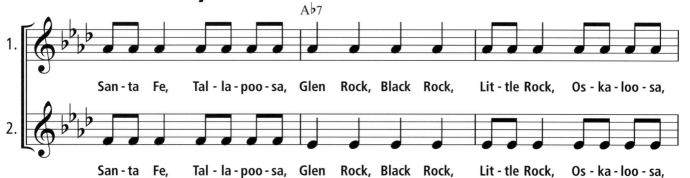

1. San - ta Fe, Tal - la - poo - sa, Glen Rock, Black Rock, Lit - tle Rock, Os - ka - loo - sa,

2. San - ta Fe, Tal - la - poo - sa, Glen Rock, Black Rock, Lit - tle Rock, Os - ka - loo - sa,

1. Ten - nes - see, Tin - ne - say, Chi - co - pee, Spir - it Lake, Grand Lake, Dev - il's Lake,

2. Ten - nes - see, Tin - ne - say, Chi - co - pee, Spir - it Lake, Grand Lake, Dev - il's Lake,

1. Cra - ter Lake, for Pete's sake! I've been ev - 'ry - where, man.

2. Cra - ter Lake, for Pete's sake! I've been ev - 'ry - where, man.

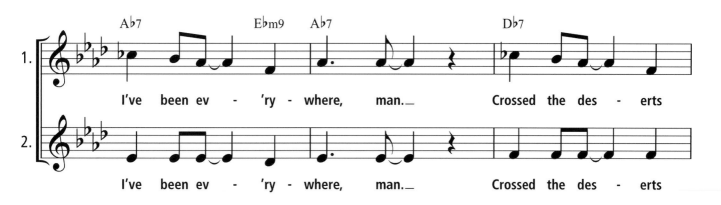

1. I've been ev - 'ry - where, man. Crossed the des - erts

2. I've been ev - 'ry - where, man. Crossed the des - erts

I've Been Everywhere

I've Been Everywhere

2. El - lens - burg, Rex - burg, Vicks - burg, El - do - ra - do,

1. Lar - i - more, At - more, Hav - er - straw, Chat - a - ni - ka,

2. Chas - ka, Ne - bras - ka, A - las - ka, Op - e - li - ka,

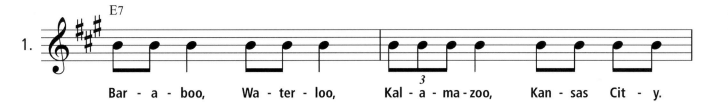

1. Bar - a - boo, Wa - ter - loo, Kal - a - ma - zoo, Kan - sas Cit - y.

2. Sioux Cit - y, Ce - dar Cit - y, Dodge Cit - y, what a pit - y!

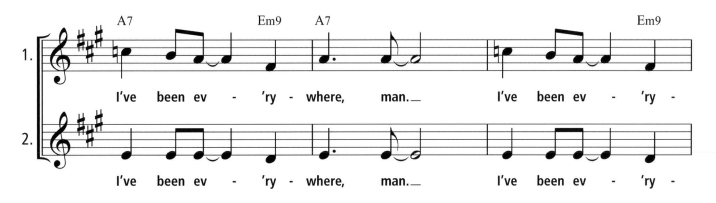

1. I've been ev - 'ry - where, man.__ I've been ev - 'ry -

2. I've been ev - 'ry - where, man.__ I've been ev - 'ry -

I've Been Everywhere

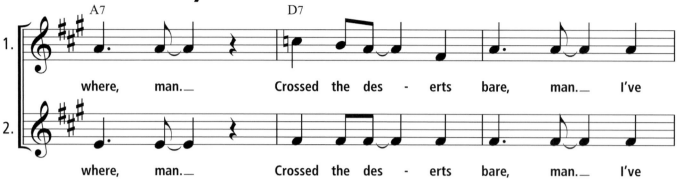

where, man.— Crossed the des - erts bare, man.— I've

where, man.— Crossed the des - erts bare, man.— I've

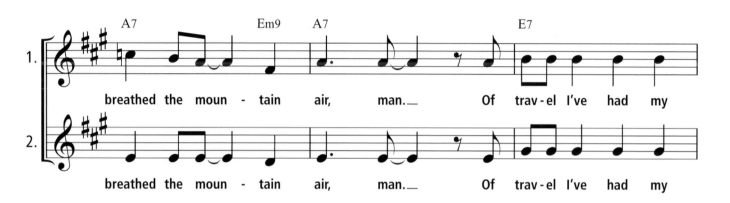

breathed the moun - tain air, man.— Of trav - el I've had my

breathed the moun - tain air, man.— Of trav - el I've had my

share, man.—— I've been ev - 'ry -

share, man.—— I've been ev - 'ry -

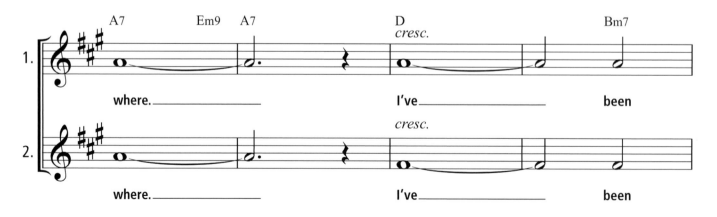

where.————— I've———— been

where.————— I've———— been

I've Been Everywhere

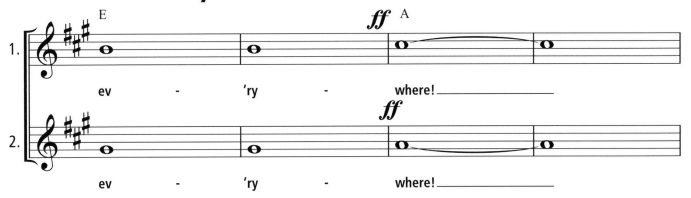

ev - 'ry - where! _____

ev - 'ry - where! _____

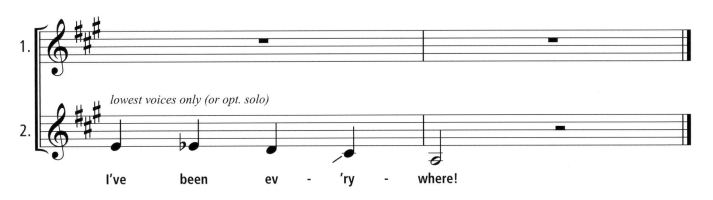

lowest voices only (or opt. solo)

I've been ev - 'ry - where!

Imbabura

Folk Song from Ecuador
English Words by Don Kalbach

1., 4. Im - ba - bu - ra de mi vi - da, tú se - rás la
1., 4. Im - ba - bu - ra, sing your prais - es, You're the best of

pre - fe - ri - da, por - que a to - dos das al - ber - gue
all the plac - es, For your shel - ter free - ly giv - en,

Fine

co - mo si fue - ran tus hi - jos.
As if we were all your chil - dren.

2. To - dos los e - cua - to - ria - nos te de - di - ca -
3. De mi co - ra - zón la due - ña has de ser, Im -
2. All the Ec - ua - do - rians love you, And they sing their
3. You have won my heart for - ev - er; It is yours, Im -

mos can - cio - nes pa - ra tus her - mo - sos
ba - bu - re - ña por - que yo ad - mi - ro tus
prais - es of you, For the beau - ty of your
ba - bu - re - ña, For I love your lakes and

1.   **2.** *D.C. al Fine*

la - gos, que nos brin - dan sus ha - la - gos.
pren - das, tus mu - jé - res y tus flo - res.
wa - ters, And de - lights that they have brought us.
wa - ters, And your peo - ple and your flow - ers.

102

Joshua Fought the Battle of Jericho

African American Spiritual

Josh - ua fought the bat - tle of_____ Jer - i - cho,_____

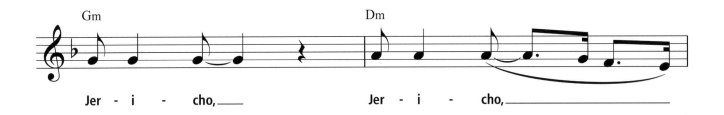

Jer - i - cho,_____ Jer - i - cho,_____

Josh - ua fought the bat - tle of_____ Jer - i - cho,_____

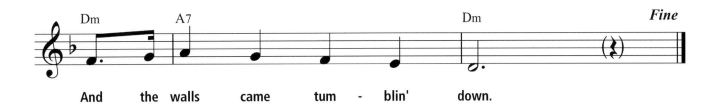

And the walls came tum - blin' down.

Joshua Fought the Battle of Jericho

B VERSE

You can talk a-bout your king of Gid - e - on,____

You can talk a - bout your man of Saul,____

But there's none like good old Josh - u - a____

Dm   A7   Dm   *D.C. al Fine*

At the bat - tle of Jer - i - cho.

Laredo

Folk Song from Mexico
English Words by Margaret Marks

do

F

1. Ya me voy pa - ra el La - re - do mi bien, Te
2. Toma e - sa lla - ví - ta de o - ro, mi bien, Abre
1. I'm off for La - re - do, fare - well, my love, I'm
2. I've bought you a hand - sewn sad - dle, my love, A

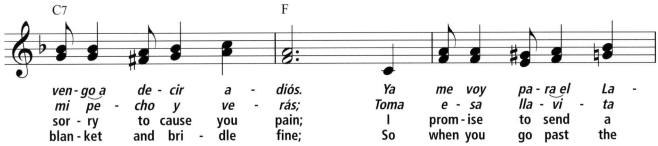

C7   F

ven - go a de - cir a - diós.   Ya me voy pa - ra el La -
mi pe - cho y ve - rás;   Toma e - sa lla - ví - ta
sor - ry to cause you pain;   I prom - ise to send a
blan - ket and bri - dle fine; So when you go past the

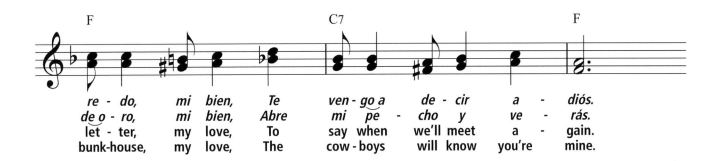

F   C7   F

re - do, mi bien, Te   ven - go a de - cir a - diós.
de o - ro, mi bien, Abre mi pe - cho y ve - rás.
let - ter, my love, To say when we'll meet a - gain.
bunk-house, my love, The cow - boys will know you're mine.

Laredo

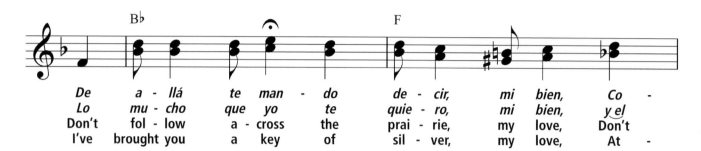

De a - llá te man - do de - cir, mi bien, Co -
Lo mu - cho que yo te quie - ro, mi bien, y el
Don't fol - low a - cross the prai - rie, my love, Don't
I've brought you a key of sil - ver, my love, At -

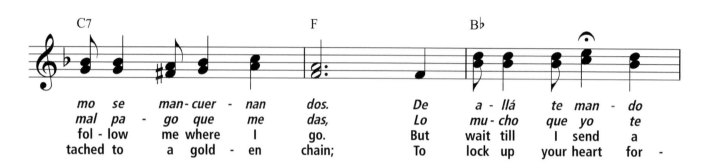

mo se man - cuer - nan dos. De a - llá te man - do
mal pa - go que me das, Lo mu - cho que yo te
fol - low me where I go. But wait till I send a
tached to a gold - en chain; To lock up your heart for -

de - cir, mi bien, Co - mo se man - cuer - nan dos.
quie - ro, mi bien, Co y el mal pa - go que me das.
mes - sage, my love, Till then I will miss you so.
e - ver, my love, If nev - er we meet a - gain.

106

Laredo

Recorder Countermelody

Laredo
Percussion

Las estrellitas del cielo
(Stars of the Heavens)

Folk Song from Mexico
English Words by Aura Kontra

do—

Las es - tre - lli - tas del cie - lo
Stars of the heav - ens are wink - ing,

Bri - llan con su luz de pla - ta.
With sil - v'ry light they are twin - kling.

San - tia - go las fué sem - bran - do
A heav - en - ly rid - er came jing - ling

Con sus es - pue - las de pla - ta.
With sil - v'ry spurs, star - light sprin - kling.

Las velitas
(Candles Burning Bright)

Folk Song from Mexico
English Words by Donald Scafuri

Her - mo - sas ve - li - tas, en la ob-scu - ri - dad.
See the lit - tle can - dles shin - ing in the night.
Ha - blan de la es -

tre - lla de la Na - vi - dad.
star with beams of ho - ly light.
Ved nues - tras ve - li - tas,
See our love - ly can - dles,

ved que a - lum - bran bien.
let them lead the way
Ha - blan de la es - tre - lla que bri - lló en Be - lén.
To a qui - et vil - lage where a ba - by lay.

Lift Ev'ry Voice and Sing

Music by J. Rosamond Johnson
Words by James Weldon Johnson

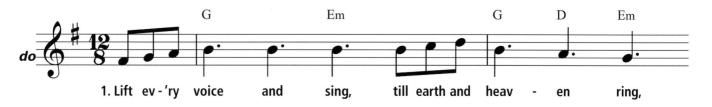

1. Lift ev-'ry voice and sing, till earth and heav - en ring,

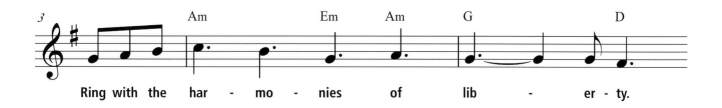

Ring with the har - mo - nies of lib - er - ty.

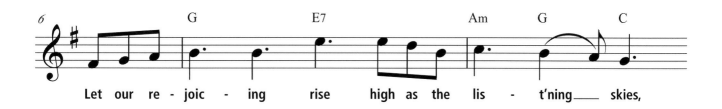

Let our re - joic - ing rise high as the lis - t'ning____ skies,

Let it re - sound loud as the roll - ing sea.

Lift Ev'ry Voice and Sing

Sing a song full of the faith that the dark past has taught us;

Sing a song full of the hope that the pres-ent has brought us;

Fac - ing the ris - ing sun of our new day be - gun,

Let us march on till vic - to - ry_____ is won.

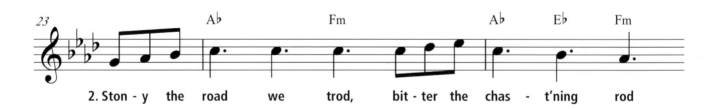

2. Ston - y the road we trod, bit - ter the chas - t'ning rod

Felt in the days when hope un - born_____ had died.

Lift Ev'ry Voice and Sing

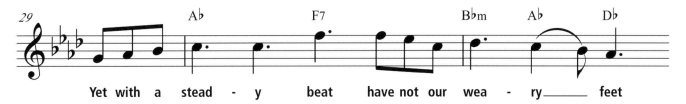

Yet with a stead - y beat have not our wea - ry feet

Come to the place for which our fa - thers died.

We have come o - ver a way that with tears has been wa - tered;

We have come tread - ing our path through the blood of the slaugh - tered;

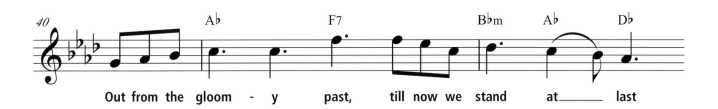

Out from the gloom - y past, till now we stand at last

Where the white gleam of our bright star is cast.

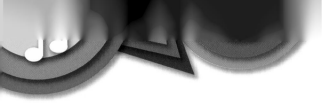

Mango Walk

Calypso Song from Jamaica

My bro - ther did - a tell me that you go man - go walk,

You go man - go walk, you go man - go walk.

My bro - ther did - a tell me that you go man - go walk

And steal all the num - ber 'lev - en.

Meng Jian Nu

Folk Song from China
English Words by Alice Firgau

Zheng yu_____ mei_____ hua, shi xing_____ the
Blos - soms from cher - ries fall, Fra - grance fills_____ the

chung,_____ Jia jia_____ hu_____ hu
air;_____ Spring - time brings__ hap - pi - ness,

tian hon_____ deng,_____ Ran_____ jia
New Year__ with - out care._____ But for me

zhang_____ fu_____ tuan yuan_____ ju,_____
there's no__ spring,__ Sad - ness__ fills my heart._____

Meng Jian Nu de__ zhang__ fu_____ zou chan_____ cheng.
Wan__ Chi Liang has__ gone a - way And now we__ are a - part._____

The Old Chisholm Trail

Cowboy Song from the United States

1. Come a - long, boys, and listen to my tale, I'll
2. I woke up one mornin' on the Chis-holm Trail, A
3. Ten dol - lar horse and a for - ty dol - lar sad - dle I'm
4. I jumped in the sad - dle and grabbed the horn,

tell you 'bout my trou - bles on the old Chis - holm Trail. Com a
rope in my hand and a cow by the tail.
read - y for punch - in' Tex - as cat - tle.
Best ole cow - boy that ev - er was born.

ti yi yip-py, yip-py yay, yip-py yay, Com a ti yi yip-py yip-py yay.

5. My seat's in the saddle and saddle's in the sky;
And I'll quit punchin' cows in the sweet by and by. *Refrain*

One Small Step

Words and Music by
Jay Althouse and Sally K. Albrecht

1. I can see a world of one great fam - i - ly
2. We must plant a seed of free - dom ev - 'ry - where.

liv - ing in peace and broth - er - hood, liv - ing in har - mo -
Nur - ture it and help it grow in un - pol - lut - ed

ny. But the world in which we live is a ver - y dif - f'rent place.
air. But a dream is still a dream un - less we do our part:

Fear and hate af - fect us all, ev - 'ry col - or, creed and
Feed the hun - gry, help the poor, giv - ing of our

race. So we must climb the walls and cross the rag - ing riv - ers. And we must
heart.

make a world of peace our com - mon goal. For we can make a dif - f'rence.

We can build a bridge and o - pen up the path - ways to our soul.

One Small Step

118

Over There

Words and Music by George M. Cohan

O - ver there, o - ver there,

Send the word, send the word o - ver there —

That the Yanks are com - ing, the Yanks are com - ing, The

drums rum tum - ming ev - 'ry - where.

So pre - pare, say a pray'r,

Send the word, send the word to be - ware.

We'll be o - ver, we're com - ing o - ver, And we

won't come back 'till it's o - ver o - ver there.

The Papaya Song

Traditional Calypso Song
Arranged by Greg Gilpin

The Papaya Song

1. If you will help me, climb up the tall tree.

2. If you will help me, climb up the tall tree.

1. Shake the pa - pa - ya down.

2. Shake the pa - pa - ya down.

all shakers play quarter notes

1. Shake the pa - pa - ya, shake them down.___

2. Shake them down, shake them down.

1. Shake the pa - pa - ya, shake them down.___

2. Shake the pa - pa - ya, shake them down.___

The Papaya Song

The Papaya Song

The Papaya Song

The Papaya Song

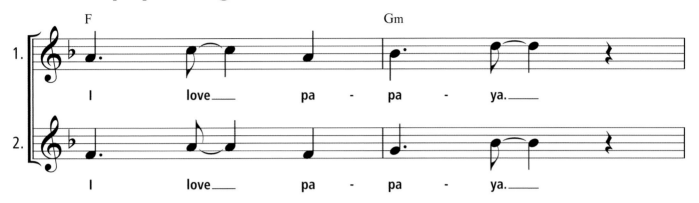

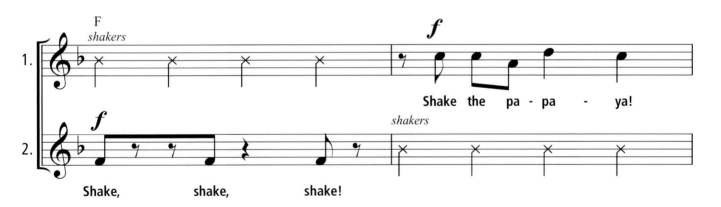

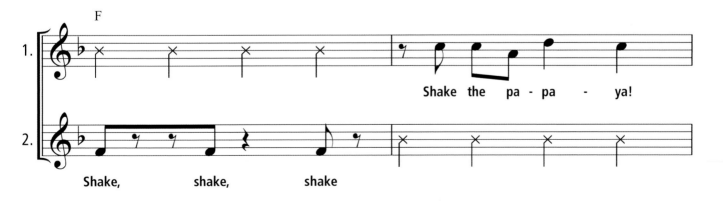

The Papaya Song

The Papaya Song

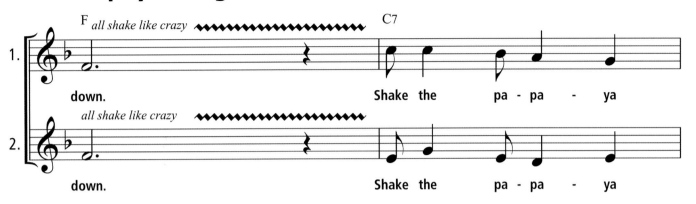

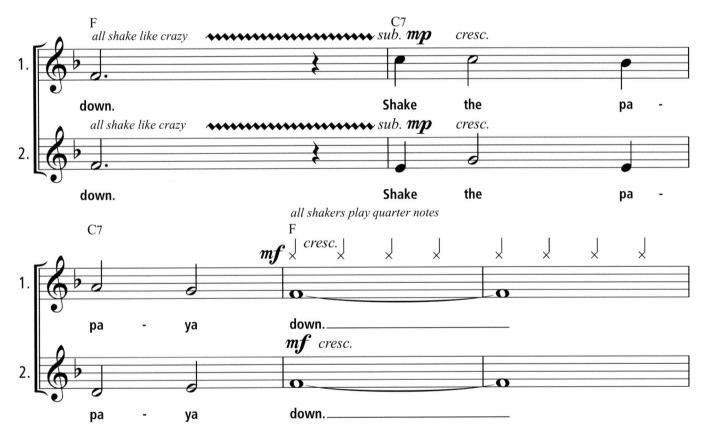

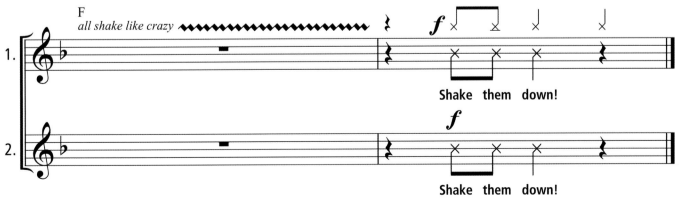

Peace Like a River

African American Spiritual

1. I've got peace like a riv-er, I've got peace like a riv-er,
2. I've got joy like a foun-tain, I've got joy like a foun-tain,
3. I've got love like the o-cean, I've got love like the o-cean,

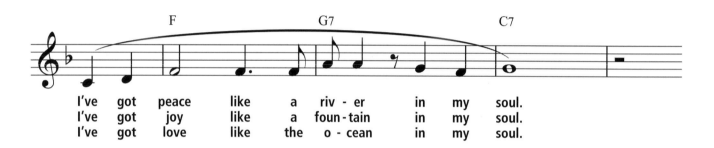

I've got peace like a riv-er in my soul.
I've got joy like a foun-tain in my soul.
I've got love like the o-cean in my soul.

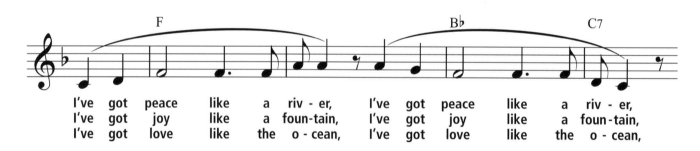

I've got peace like a riv-er, I've got peace like a riv-er,
I've got joy like a foun-tain, I've got joy like a foun-tain,
I've got love like the o-cean, I've got love like the o-cean,

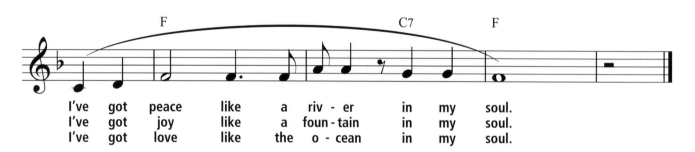

I've got peace like a riv-er in my soul.
I've got joy like a foun-tain in my soul.
I've got love like the o-cean in my soul.

¡Qué bonita bandera!
(What a Beautiful Banner!)

Folk Song from Puerto Rico
English Words by Samuel Maqui

VERSE

A - zul, blan - ca y___ co - lo - ra - da, y en el
Blue and white and red___ are the col - ors, with a

me - dio tie - ne un es - tre - lla. Bo - ni - ta, se -
pure white star in the cen - ter. A beau - ti - ful

ñor - es, es la ban - de - ra Puer - to - ri - qeu - ña.
ban - ner is the flag of our Puer - to Ri - co!

REFRAIN

¡Qué bo - ni - ta ban - de - ra! ¡Qué bo - ni - ta ban - de - ra!
What a beau - ti - ful ban - ner! What a beau - ti - ful ban - ner!

¡Qué bo - ni - ta ban - de - ra es la ban - de - ra Puer - to - ri - que - ña!
What a beau - ti - ful ban - ner is the flag of our Puer - to Ri - co!

129

Ragupati Ragava Raja Ram

Traditional Melody
Traditional Hindu Song

REFRAIN

Ra - gu - pa - ti   ra - ga - va   ra - ja____ Ram____

gradual accelerando

Pa - ti - ta   pa - va - na   Si - ta____ Ram.

VERSE

1. Si - ta   Ram   jai   Si - ta____ Ram,
2. Ish - ware   Al - lah   te - re____ nam,

Pa - ti - ta   pa - va - na   Si - ta____ Ram.
Sub - be - ko   sun - mut - ti   de   bha - ga - wan.

Río, río
(River, River)

Traditional Song from Chile
English Words by Alice Firgau

do

F

Qué gran - de que vie - ne el rí - o, _____ qué
How wide _____ and deep is the riv - er, _____ How

C7

C7

gran - de se va a la mar. _____
swift - ly it flows to the sea. _____

F

C7

Si lo au - men - ta el _____ llan - to
Rí - o, rí - o, _____ rí - o,
Riv - er, riv - er, _____ flow - ing

F

C7

F

mí - o _____ co - mo gran - de _____ no ha de es - tar, _____ Si lo au -
rí - o, _____ De - vol - ved - me el _____ a - mor mí - o. De - vol -
wa - ters, _____ Oh, how deep it _____ then would be. If my

a tempo

C7

F

C7

F

men - ta el llan - to mí - o _____ co - mo gran - de _____ no ha de es - tar.
ved - me el a - mor mí - o _____ que me can - so de llo - rar.
tears should meet its wa - ters, _____ Oh, how deep it _____ then would be.
turn my _____ love to me, Oh, _____ from my sor - row _____ set me free.

131

Shenandoah

Capstan Sea Shanty

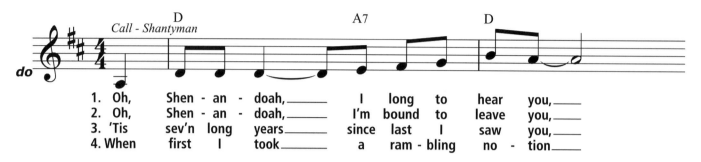

Call - Shantyman

	D			A7			D		

1. Oh, Shen - an - doah, _____ I long to hear you, _____
2. Oh, Shen - an - doah, _____ I'm bound to leave you, _____
3. 'Tis sev'n long years _____ since last I saw you, _____
4. When first I took _____ a ram - bling no - tion _____

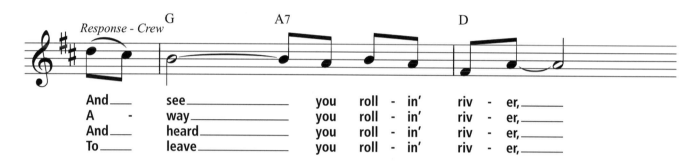

Response - Crew

G		A7			D		

And _____ see _____ you roll - in' riv - er, _____
A - way _____ you roll - in' riv - er, _____
And _____ heard _____ you roll - in' riv - er, _____
To _____ leave _____ you roll - in' riv - er, _____

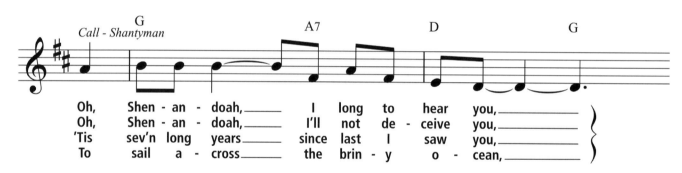

Call - Shantyman

G		A7		D		G

Oh, Shen - an - doah, _____ I long to hear you, _____
Oh, Shen - an - doah, _____ I'll not de - ceive you, _____
'Tis sev'n long years _____ since last I saw you, _____
To sail a - cross _____ the brin - y o - cean, _____

Response - Crew

D			A7	D

A - way, _____ I'm bound a - way, 'Cross the wide _____ Mis-sou - ri.

Shenandoah

Recorder Countermelody

Simple Gifts

Shaker Song

'Tis the gift to be sim - ple, 'Tis the gift to be free, 'Tis the gift to come down where we ought to be, And when we find our - selves in the place just right, 'Twill be in the val - ley of love and de - light. When true sim - pli - ci - ty is gained, To bow and to bend we shan't be a - shamed, To turn, turn will be our de - light, Till by turn - ing, turn - ing we come 'round right.

134

Simple Gifts

Recorder Countermelody

Sing Me a Song

Words and Music by Leonard Enns
Arranged by Michael Story

do- Come on and sing me a song.___ it makes the
sun shine___ bright - er,___ sing me a song___ if there's a
rain; just take the time for a song,___ and make my
heart much___ light - er,___ bring that smile a -
gain. Come sing me a song,___ it makes the
sun shine___ bright - er,___ sing me a song___ if there's a

Sing Me a Song

Sing, Sing, Sing!

Words and Music by Louis Prima

Singin' in the Rain

Music by Nacio Herb Brown
Lyrics by Arthur Freed
Arranged, with New Words and Music, by Sally K. Albrecht

1st time: PART I only
2nd time: PART II only
3rd time: Sing both parts

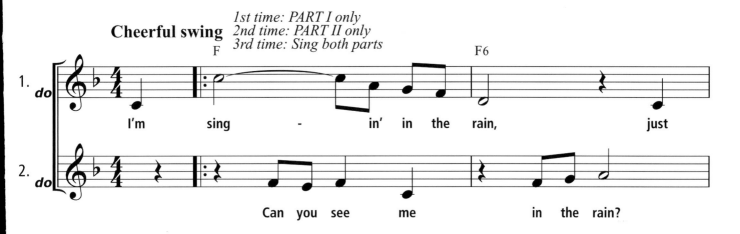

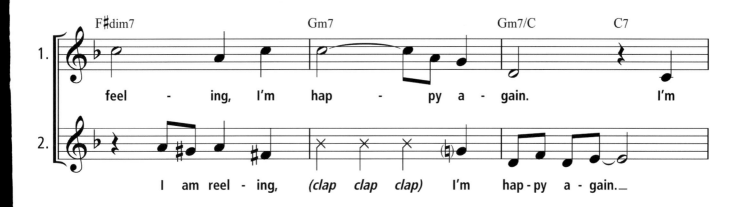

Singin' in the Rain

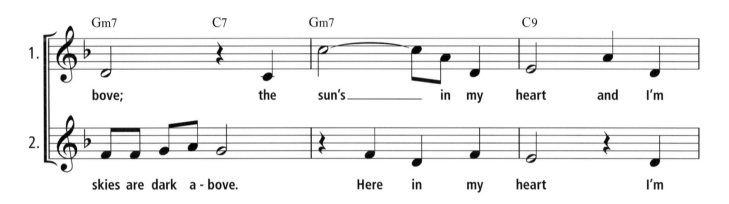

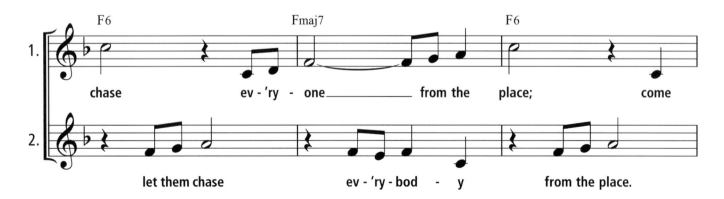

Singin' in the Rain

Singin' in the Rain

Recorder Countermelody

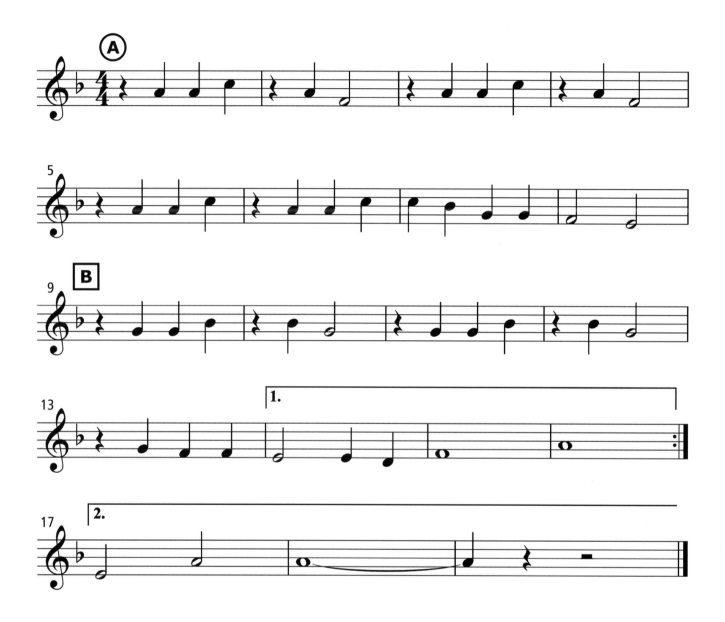

Solfège Song

Words and Music by Andy Beck

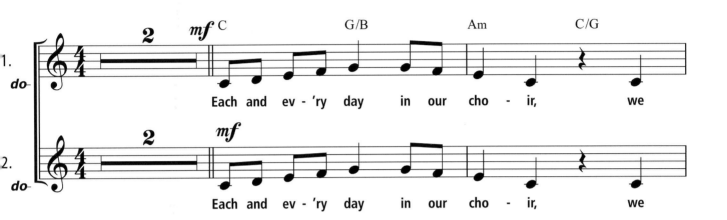

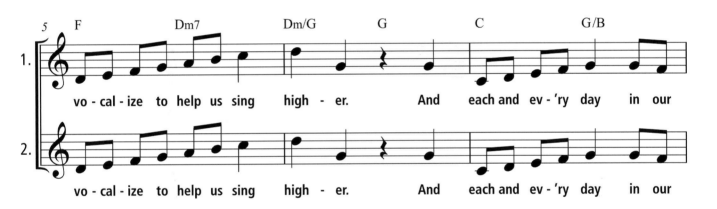

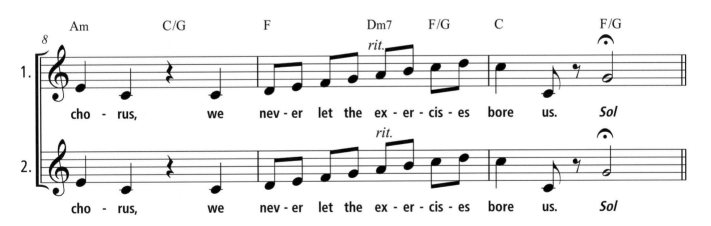

Solfège Song

1st time: PART 1 only
2nd time: PART 2 only

Solfège Song

Solfège Song

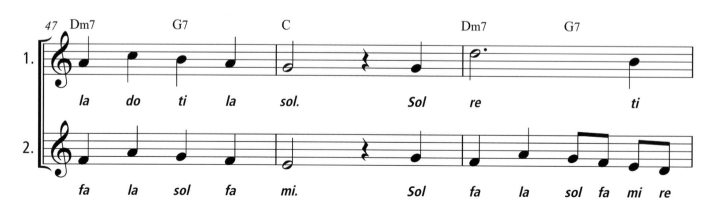

Solfège Song

Solfège Song

148

The Star-Spangled Banner

Music by John Stafford Smith
Words by Francis Scott Key

1. Oh, — say! can you see, — by the dawn's ear - ly light,
2. On the shore, dim - ly seen — through the mists of the deep,
3. Oh, — thus be it ev - er when — free men shall stand

What so proud - ly we hailed at the twi - light's last gleam - ing,
Where the foe's haugh-ty host in dread si - lence re - pos - es,
Be - tween their loved homes and the war's des - o - la - tion!

Whose broad stripes and bright stars, through the per - il - ous fight,
What is that which the breeze, o'er the tow - er - ing steep,
Blest with vict - 'ry and peace, may the heav'n - res - cued land

O'er the ram - parts we watched were so gal - lant - ly stream - ing?
As it fit - ful - ly blows, half con - ceals, half dis - clos - es?
Praise the Pow'r that hath made and pre - served us a na - tion!

149

The Star-Spangled Banner

And the rock - et's red glare, the bombs burst - ing in air,
Now it catch - es the gleam of the morn - ing's first beam,
Then— con - quer we must, for our cause it is just,

Gave proof through the night— that our flag was still there.
In full glo - ry re - flect - ed now— shines on the stream.
And this be our mot - to: "In— God is our trust!"

Oh, say, does that Star - Span - gled Ban - ner— yet— wave—
'Tis the Star - Span - gled Ban - ner, oh, long may it— wave—
And the Star - Span - gled Ban - ner in tri - umph shall wave—

O'er the land_____ of the free and the home of the brave?
O'er the land_____ of the free and the home of the brave!
O'er the land_____ of the free and the home of the brave!

Still, Still, Still
(Sleep, Dearest Child)

Traditional Carol from Austria
English Words by Ruth Martin (adapted)

1. Still,____ still,____ still, weils__ Kind - lein__ schla - fen__
2. Schlaf,____ schlaf,____ schlaf, mein__ lie - bes__ Kind - lein__
1. Sleep,____ sleep,____ sleep, my__ dear - est__ child, now__
2. Dream,____ dream,____ dream, a__ love - ly__ shin - ing__

will. Ma - ri - a____ tut es nie - der - sing - en,
schlaf. Die Eng - el____ tun schön mu - si - zie - ren
sleep. The guard - ian____ an - gels dear - ly____ love you,
dream. A - cross the____ deep blue heav - ens____ yon - der,

sei - ne____ gro - sse Lieb dar - bring - en.
bei dem____ Kind - lein ju - bi - lie - ren.
Sing - ing____ soft - ly there a - bove you.
Light - ly from star to star you'll____ wan - der.

Still,____ still,____ still, weils Kind - lein__ schla - fen__ will.
Schlaf,_ schlaf,_ schlaf, mein_ lie - bes__ Kind - lein__ schlaf.
Sleep,_ sleep,_ sleep, my__ dear - est__ child, now__ sleep.
Dream,_ dream,_ dream, a__ love - ly____ shin - ing__ dream.

Strike Up the Band!

Music and Lyrics by George Gershwin and Ira Gershwin
Arranged, with New Words and Music, by Sally K. Albrecht

1st time: PART 1 only
2nd time: PART 2 only
3rd time: Both parts

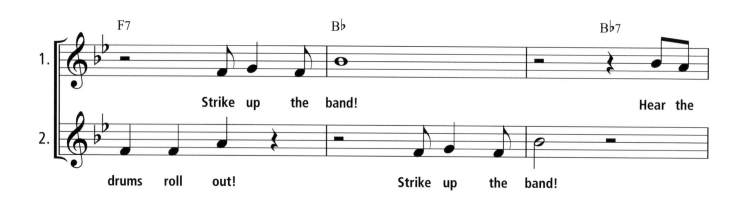

Strike Up the Band!

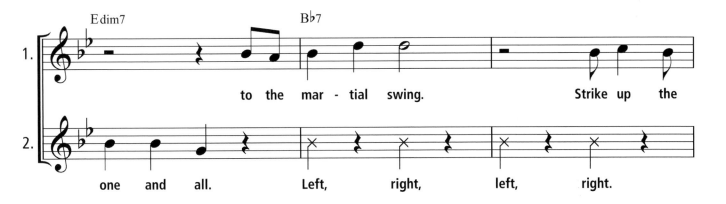

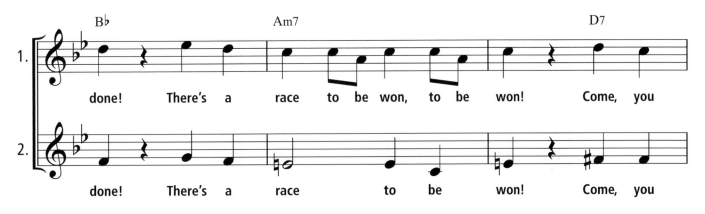

Strike Up the Band!

Tama tu
(A Maori Proverb)

Words and Music by
Sally K. Albrecht

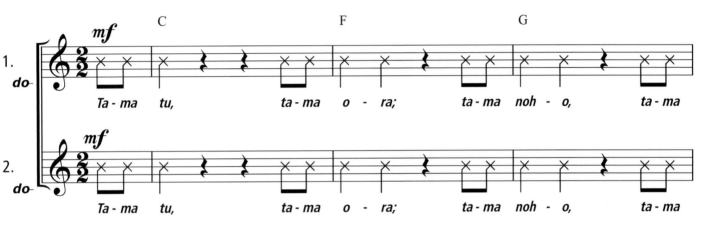

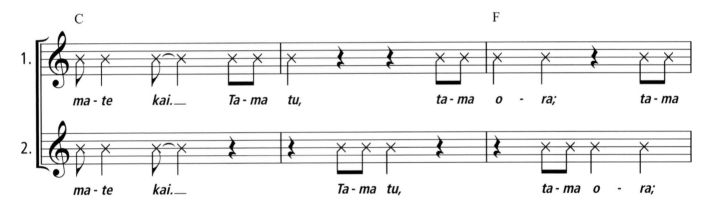

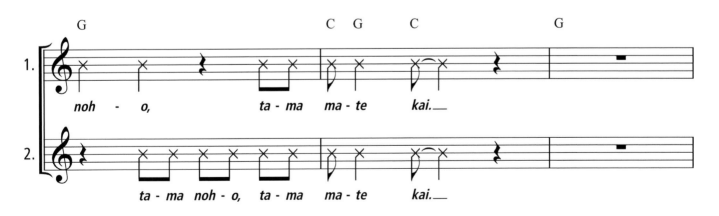

Tama tu

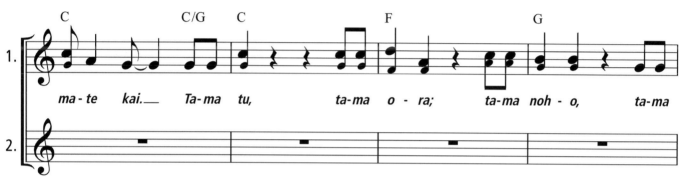

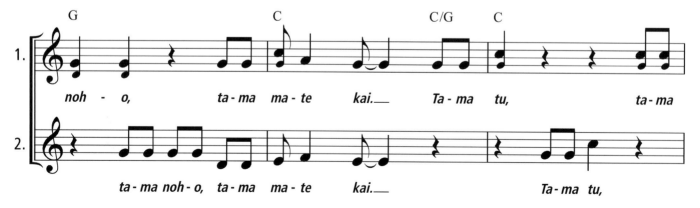

Tama tu

o - ra;   ta - ma noh - o,   ta - ma ma - te   kai.

ta - ma o - ra;   ta - ma noh - o, ta - ma ma - te   kai.

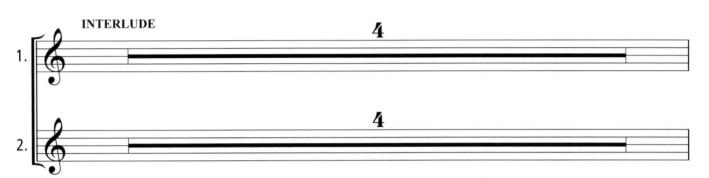

INTERLUDE

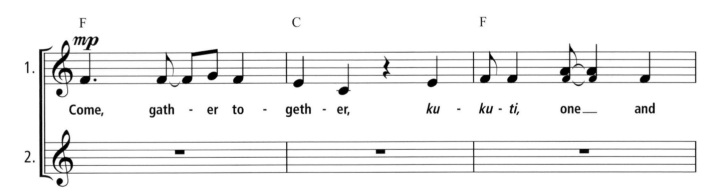

Come,   gath - er to - geth - er,   ku - ku - ti,   one   and

all.

Now is   the time,   po   a - ta   ra - u.

Tama tu

Tama tu

Tama tu

Tama tu

Tancovačka
(Dancing)

Slovak Folk Song

VERSE

Tan - cuj, tan - cuj, vy - krú - caj, vy - krú - caj,
Come and dance, turn light - ly, turn light - ly A -

Len mi pie - cku ne - zrú - caj, ne - zrú - caj.
round the camp - fire burn - ing so bright - ly. The

Do - brá pie - cka na zi - mu, na zi - mu,
snow falls fast and cold is the weath - er. Come

Keď ne - má - me pe - ri - nu, pe - ri - nu.
dance, come dance, we'll___ all turn to - geth - er.

162

Tancovačka

This Train

African American Spiritual

1. This train is bound for glo - ry, this train.
2. This train don't pull no sleep - ers, this train.
3. This train don't take your mon - ey, this train.

This train is bound for glo - ry, this train.
This train don't pull no sleep - ers, this train.
This train don't take your mon - ey, this train.

This train is bound for glo - ry, don't car - ry none but the good and ho - ly.
This train don't pull no sleep - ers, don't pull nothin' but the right - eous peo - ple.
This train don't take your mon - ey, pay your way with milk and hon - ey.

This train is bound for glo - ry, this train.

Tumba

Hebrew Melody

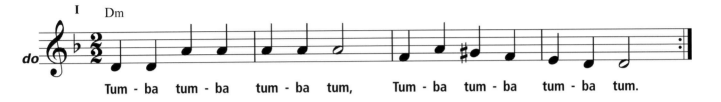

Tum - ba tum - ba tum - ba tum,   Tum - ba tum - ba tum - ba tum.

La la la la la la,   La la la la la,   La la la la la la,   La la la la.

Tum - ba,   Tum - ba,   Tum - ba.

Turn the Beat Around

*Words and Music by
Peter Jackson, Jr. and Gerald Jackson*

Turn it up, turn it up, turn it up - side down.

Turn the beat_ a - round._ Love to hear_ per - cus - sion.

Turn it up - side down._ Love to hear_ per - cus - sion.

Love to hear_ it. 1. Blow, horns, you sure sound pret - ty. Your vi - o - lins keep

mov - in' to the nit - ty grit - ty. When you hear the scratch of the gui - tar scratch-

- ing, then you know that rhy - thm cor - ners all the ac - tion, whoa_ yeah.

Turn the Beat Around

Turn the Beat Around

Twelve Gates to the City

African American Spiritual

Oh, _____ what a beau - ti - ful ci - ty; _____ Oh, _____ what a

beau - ti - ful ci - ty; _____ Oh, _____ what a beau - ti - ful ci - ty; _____

Fine
2nd time to Refrain
3rd time to Verse 2

Twelve gates_ to the ci - ty, a - hal - le - lu. _____

VERSE

1. My Lord built_____ the ci - ty, _____ Ci - ty was just_____ four

square, Said he want - ed his child - ren_____ to

meet him in_____ the air, And there's twelve gates_ to the

169

Twelve Gates to the City

ci - ty, a - hal - le - lu.

2. Three gates in - a the East,___ Three gates in - a the West,

___ Three gates in___ the North,___

Three gates in - a the South,___ That makes twelve gates_ to the

ci - ty, a - hal - le - lu.

'Ūlili E

Traditional Song from Hawaii
Arranged by Wanda Gereben

1. Ho - ne a - na ko le - o e 'ū - li - li e E - ka - hi
2. Ho - ne a - na ko le - o e kō - le - a e Pe - he - a

ma - nu__ no - ho a - 'e kai Ki - a - 'i ma ka lae o__ Ke - u
'o Ka - hi - ki? Mai - ka - 'i no. 'O - i - a 'āi - na u - lu - we - hi -

ka - ha 'O - i - a kai u - a la - na ma - li - e. 'Ū - li - li
we - hi I hu - i pū 'i - a me ke o - nao - na.

'A - ha - ha - na 'ū - li - li 'e - he - he - ne 'ū - li - li 'a - ha - ha - na__

'ū - li - li ho - 'i__

'E - he - he - ne 'ū - li - li 'a - ha - ha - na 'ū - li - li 'e - he - he - ne__

'Ulili E

'Ū - li - li   ho - lo   ho - lo   ka - ha - kai____ e,

'O - i - a   kai   u - a   la - na   ma -

1.

2.

li - e.   'Ū - li - li   li - e.____

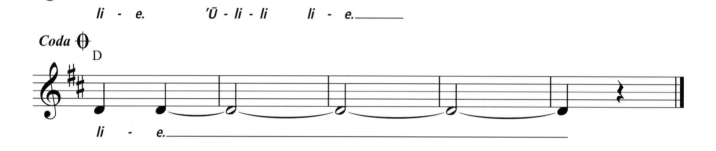

Coda

li - e.____

172

Wabash Cannon Ball

Traditional

1. From the coast of the At - lan - tic to the wide Pa - ci - fic shore,
2. There are ci - ties of im - por - tance that are reached a - long the way,

From the warm and sun - ny South-land to the isle of Lab - ra - dor,
Chi - ca - go and Saint Lou - is and Rock Is - land, San - ta Fe,

There's a name of great im - por - tance that is known by one and all,
And Spring - field and De - ca - tur and Pe - or - ia, Mon - tre - al,

It's the West - ern com - bi - na - tion called the *Wa - bash Can - non* Ball.
On the West - ern com - bi - na - tion called the *Wa - bash Can - non* Ball.

Wabash Cannon Ball

REFRAIN

Just lis - ten to the jin - gle, the rum - ble, and the roar

Of the might - y lo - co - mo - tive as she streams a - long the shore,

Hear the thun - der of the en - gine, hear the lone - some whis - tle call,

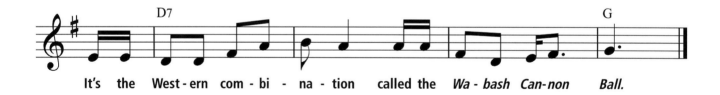

It's the West - ern com - bi - na - tion called the *Wa - bash Can - non Ball.*

Wabash Cannon Ball

Recorder Countermelody

Wabash Cannon Ball

Rhythm: Reading

Watoto Wa Dunia
(Children of the Earth—Swahili)

Words and Music by
Sally K. Albrecht and Jay Althouse

Watoto Wa Dunia

1. Chil-dren of the world, don't let time slip a - way.

2. Chil-dren of the world, don't let time slip a - way.

1. Ku - ji - u - nga pa - mo - ja, to - geth - er as one. Ku -

2. Ku - ji - u - nga pa - mo - ja, to - geth - er as one. Ku -

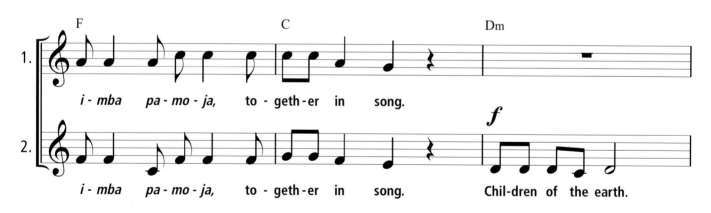

1. i - mba pa - mo - ja, to - geth - er in song.

2. i - mba pa - mo - ja, to - geth - er in song. Chil-dren of the earth.

1. Chil-dren of the earth. Chil-dren of the earth, we are

2. Chil-dren of the earth, we are

178

Watoto Wa Dunia

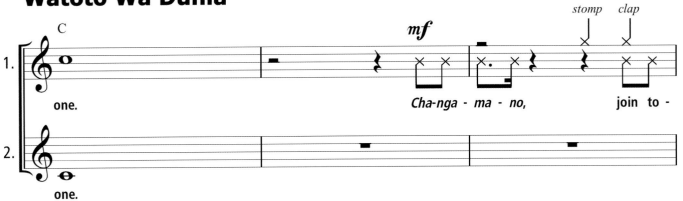

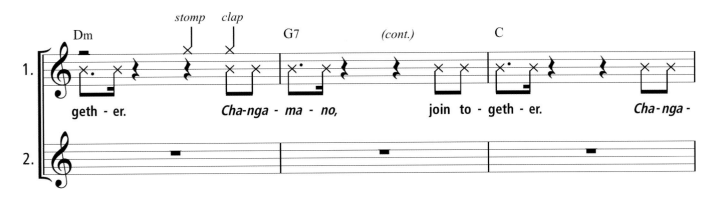

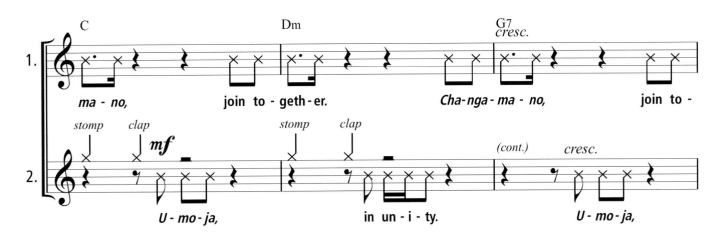

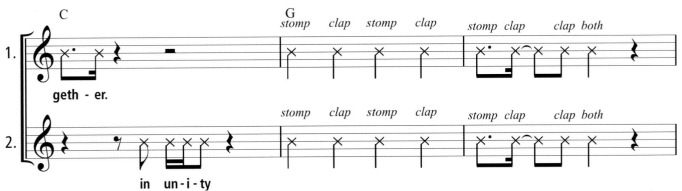

Watoto Wa Dunia

1. Chil-dren of the earth, treas-ure life each day.

2. Chil-dren of the earth, treas-ure life each day.

1. Chil-dren of the world, don't let

2. Chil-dren of the world, don't let

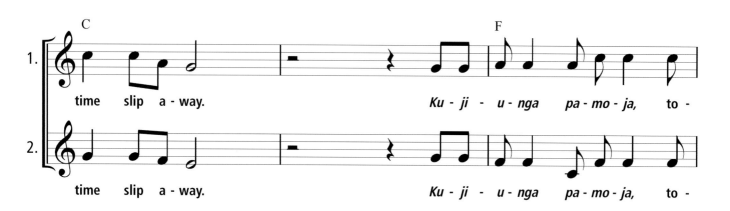

1. time slip a-way. Ku - ji - u - nga pa - mo - ja, to -

2. time slip a-way. Ku - ji - u - nga pa - mo - ja, to -

1. geth-er as one. Ku - i - mba pa - mo - ja, to - geth-er in song.

2. geth-er as one. Ku - i - mba pa - mo - ja, to - geth-er in song.

180

Watoto Wa Dunia

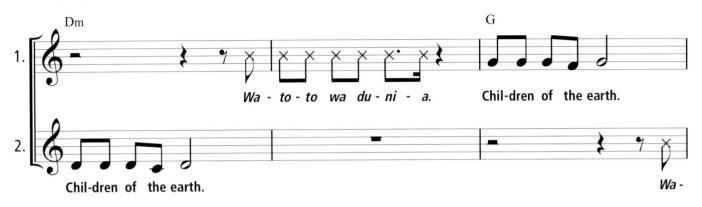

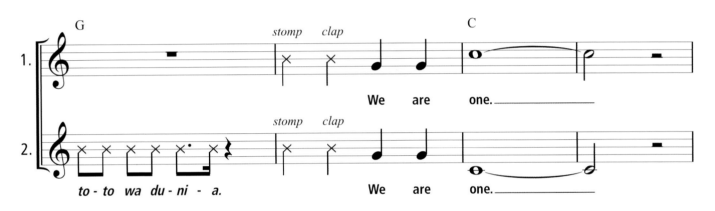

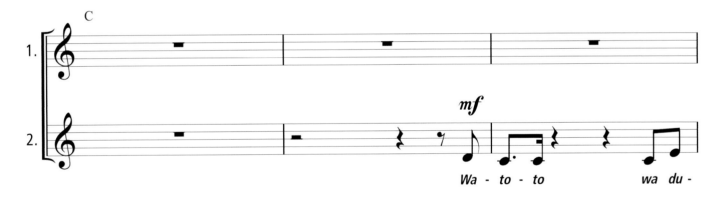

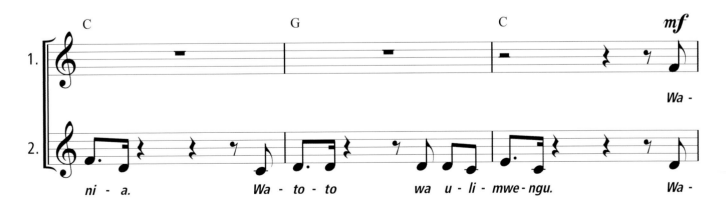

Watoto Wa Dunia

When Johnny Comes Marching Home

Words and Music by Patrick S. Gilmore

1. When John - ny comes march - ing home a - gain, Hur - rah! Hur - rah!
2. Let love and friend - ship on that day,
3. Get read - y for the ju - bi - lee,

We'll give him a heart - y wel - come then, Hur - rah! Hur - rah!
Their choic - est trea - sure then dis - play,
We'll give the he - ro three times three,

The men will cheer, the boys will shout, The la - dies they will all turn out,
And let each one per - form some part, To fill with joy the war - rior's heart,
The laur - el wreath is read - y now To place up - on his roy - al brow,

And we'll shout "Hur - rah" when John - ny comes march - ing home!

Winter Wonderland

Words by Dick Smith
Music by Felix Bernard

Winter Wonderland

snow - man, then pretend that he is Par - son Brown.

He'll say, "Are you mar - ried?" We'll say, "No man, but

you can do the job when you're in town!" Lat - er on, we'll con-

spire, __ as we dream by the fire, __ to face un - a - fraid, __ the

plans that we made, __ walk - in' in a win - ter won - der - land.

185

Zum gali gali

Folk Song from Israel
English Words by David Eddleman

REFRAIN

Em

Zum ga - li, ga - li, ga - li, zum ga - li, ga - li,

Em — Fine

Zum ga - li, ga - li, ga - li, zum ga - li, ga - li.

VERSE

Em — D — Em

1. He - cha - lutz le 'man a - vo - dah; A - vo - dah le
2. He - cha - lutz le 'man ha - b'tu - lah; Ha - b'tu - lah le
1. We are build - ing, build - ing a land, Out of rock and
2. So that war and hun - ger may cease, We are work - ing,

D — Em — D — Em

'man he - cha - lutz. A - vo - dah le 'man he - cha - lutz.
'man he - cha - lutz; Ha - sha - lom le 'man ha' a - mim;
de - sert and sand; Men and wo - men la - bor in pride,
work - ing for peace. Though the days be heav - y and long,

Em — D — Em — D.C. al Fine

He - cha - lutz le 'man a - vo - dah.
Ha' - a - mim le 'man ha - sha - lom.
We are work - ing side by_____ side.
We will make our na - tion_____ strong.

186

Index